ANOTHER WORLD
IS POSSIBLE IF ...

ANOTHER WORLD IS POSSIBLE IF ...

◆

SUSAN GEORGE

V

VERSO

London • New York

Published in association with the Transnational Institute

The Transnational Institute (TNI) was founded in 1974 as a worldwide fellowship of committed scholar-activists co-ordinated from Amsterdam. In the spirit of public scholarship, and aligned to no political party, TNI seeks to create and promote transnational co-operation in analysing and finding possible solutions to the global problems of today and tomorrow. Much of its work is geared to providing intellectual support to those movements concerned to steer the world in a democratic, equitable and environmentally sustainable direction.

First published by Verso 2004
© Susan George 2004
All rights reserved

1 3 5 7 9 10 8 6 4 2

Verso
UK: 6 Meard Street, London W1F 0EG
USA: 180 Varick Street, New York, NY 10014–4606
www.versobooks.com

Verso is the imprint of New Left Books

ISBN 1–84467–510–6

British Library Cataloguing in Publication Data
George, Susan
    Another world is possible if
    1. World politics – 20th century 2. World politics –
    21st century 3. International relations
    I. Title
    909.8'2
    ISBN 1844675106

Library of Congress Cataloging-in-Publication Data
George, Susan.
    Another world is possible if– / Susan George.
    p. cm.
    ISBN 1-84467-510-6 (pbk. : alk. paper)
    1. Social action. 2. Social change. 3. Social policy.
    4. Social justice. 5. Globalization. I. Title.
    HN18.3.G46 2004

    303.4–dc22

                                        2004010012

Typeset in Garamond
Printed in the USA by R. R. Donnelley & Sons

CONTENTS

INTRODUCTION

Journalists tend to call the people who take part in mass demonstrations the "anti-globalisation movement." Those concerned refer to themselves collectively as the "social movement," the "citizens' movement" or the "global justice movement." In a pinch, if headline space is really at a premium, they'll settle for "alter-" or "counter-," as preferable to the inaccurate, even insulting, "anti-"globalisation. The movement is not "anti" but internationalist and deeply engaged with the world as a whole and the fate of everyone who shares the planet. It also has plenty of concrete proposals to offer, making it easily more "pro-globalisation" than its adversaries. It all depends on what kind of globalisation one means, and for whom.

People who feel themselves part of this movement may be a wildly disparate lot, but if there's one thing that unites them it's the belief that "another world is possible." This popular slogan appears on posters, banners and T-shirts; people like me end their rally speeches with it, and Brazilians, being Brazilians, have turned it into a samba, "Um outro mundo é possível." But is it? I believe the answer is yes, *if* …

This book is devoted to exploring those two letters which can transform everything.

When I joined the "movement" as it was then called, without adjectives, in the late 1960s, you could say (or shout) "US get out of Vietnam" and everyone knew what you were talking about. Thirty-five years later, if you say – little point in shouting – "Impose a moratorium on the GATS" or "Abolish structural adjustment," you're likely to get a blank stare. Getting to another possible world now requires particularly well-informed citizens.

I hope that seasoned campaigners and experienced world-changers may also find this book useful, but at least part of it is a kind of "Globalisation and the Global Justice Movement for Beginners." The gap between knowledge and politics is widening, and many people seem to feel that they can't participate in a politics of transformation even when they recognise the desperate need to do so.

Mounting rates of abstention in national elections show that many also see little point in representative democracy. They are disgusted with traditional politicians: "they're all the same" or, worse, "they're all corrupt." Or they simply see politicians and party politics as irrelevant. Refusing to have anything to do with public life, they prefer to retreat into their private concerns.

The trouble with that attitude is that those private concerns can no longer be separated – if they ever could – from the outside world and the larger sphere which envelops them. Politics insinuates itself into all our lives. Increasingly, problems can no longer be solved individually, locally or even nationally because globalisation is more than a slogan or an ideology; it's also a transfer of power to such a lofty level that citizens' voices sound faint and far away. Realising this implicitly or explicitly, people may feel even more frustrated and powerless, retreat even more and so on, in a vicious spiral.

This book tries to make sense of that larger sphere and higher level. It's addressed to the great number of people who hope and believe that change is possible and are already working to bring it about. Until you become active in the global justice movement, you have no idea how many fantastically smart, courageous and energetic people believe the same things you do and are willing to fight for them – such, at least, has been my fortunate experience.

It's also for those who are hesitant and doubtful that anything can be done as well as for those unsure how to take the plunge. Those who simply want to understand the global justice movement as a new political phenomenon and as an actor on the world stage may also find it useful insofar as this book explains what makes it – and us – tick: our motives, our worldviews, our hopes and our goals.

It's for the people who have raised their hands in the discussion after one of my talks saying, "This is probably a stupid question but...." (Wrong: no question is stupid and a lot of phenomena *are* hard to figure out.) It's dedicated to the three obviously bright *lycée* students who told me, "We read the Attac* manifesto and didn't understand it"; to the woman who admitted she had given up going to meetings of her local alter-globalisation group because she couldn't follow the conversations. It's for the many who express their fury and revulsion at conventional politics but see no alternative, as

---

* Just a quick note here: Attac, "an action-oriented popular education movement," was founded in France (where I am currently one of the vice-presidents) in 1998 and in mid-2003 existed in fifty-one countries. The name stands for Association to Tax financial Transactions to Aid Citizens; that is, tax financial markets and transnational corporations in order to redistribute income globally. Attac fights against third-world debt and tax havens and demands complete restructuring of major international institutions (World Bank, International Monetary Fund and World Trade Organisation) in order to move towards greater global justice. More on the programme later.

well as for that famous and doubtless mythical creature, the average citizen, who doubles as the "intelligent, non-specialised reader."

Whether you're among the latter or an experienced campaigner, if you've read this far you are probably, like me, dismayed by the wild gyrations of the world economy, shocked by daily evidence of corruption in high places and sick of seeing major corporations "mislay" billions of dollars with the connivance of their auditors, bankers and putative government watchdogs. You see unemployment and casual work increasing, with young people especially hard hit; you know the environment is on the brink of collapse and climate change threatens us all with devastating heatwaves, storms, floods, crop failures, untold disruption – perhaps even extinction.

You're worried about the growing poverty of hundreds of millions and think it's connected to terrorism and war. You've watched the ambitions of the only hyper-super-mega-power run out of control, particularly in a war millions tried to prevent and whose long-term consequences remain to be seen.

In a word, you can see that globalisation is already having a largely negative impact on you, your family, friends and community, on the economy and society of your country, on world peace and security and on the planet at large.

Are all these processes impossible to control? Can citizens' opinions still make a difference? What, as the old question goes, is to be done?

My answer is that another world is indeed possible – but only with the greatest possible number of people with many backgrounds, viewpoints and skills joining together to make it happen. Things change when enough people insist on it and work for it. No one should be left out or feel that they cannot contribute. No one who wants to help build another world should, for lack of knowledge or connections, remain on the sidelines.

I shall attempt modestly to provide some of the knowledge and the connections. No prior acquaintance with economics or any other discipline is required, fortunately enough for me since I'm not an economist. But I do poach a lot on their territory so I know what it's like to cross their bleak steppes and hack though their dense jungles in search of explanations. This journey has helped me to understand people who believe, wrongly, that they can neither comprehend nor influence the way the world works today. I guarantee they can do both.

Another world is also possible if we avoid some common mistakes, choose the right targets and apply to them the right strategies. I certainly do not pretend to supply here all the answers, but perhaps my experience as a writer, speaker and campaigner for change over several decades may qualify me at least to ask some pertinent questions and point to some pathways as well as make some cautionary remarks. In the following pages, I don't hesitate to refer to this personal experience when I believe it may be useful to others.

Many answers can only be collectively arrived at through democratic debate because we face an historically unprecedented moment. No one has ever tried to democratise the international space before, or to ensure a decent existence for everyone on earth. These goals are no longer utopian but have become practical prospects; whence the declaration that another world is possible, because it really is.

I thank those who have thanked me after a talk for "being so clear," giving me hope that I may also be clear in writing.

The views expressed throughout are my own and do not necessarily reflect those of Attac, the Transnational Institute or any other organisation.

PART ONE

ANOTHER WORLD IS POSSIBLE IF...

1

... WE KNOW WHAT WE'RE TALKING ABOUT

"GLOBALISATION" AND OTHER LIES

When journalists ask me for interviews on the "anti-globalisation movement," I first ask them politely please not to call it that. Then I try to explain what we mean by *neo-liberal* globalisation. I'll first try to clarify what movement participants are talking about by sorting out some terms and defining what we place under the general heading of globalisation.

Sometimes it seems that every other day someone sends me a book with that dreaded word in the title. Like flowers in springtime and apples in autumn, abundant resources on the topic are there for the picking, but a lot of nonsense gets spread about as well. I shall try not to contribute any more of it, just to put up a few guideposts and make some remarks with no pretensions to being exhaustive.

In a speech delivered in 2002, German President Johannes Rau said that at the end of the 1990s half the German population had never heard of globalisation, but by 2002 virtually everyone in his country knew this word. I did find the French equivalent *mondialisation* in the 1980 *Larousse*, but globalisation isn't in the 1976 Oxford English Dictionary. Today, this hugely overworked and invasive word is all over the place. So what does it mean?

Actually, by itself it doesn't mean much, and we may as well start there. It's always healthy to examine critically the vocabulary that serves to describe – and just as often to obfuscate or camouflage – any phenomenon. People have a right, in fact a duty, to insist on definitions. What if someone glibly tells you that several hundred job losses in your town are "due to globalisation" and it's hopeless to fight back because "globalisation is irreversible" and one must "adjust" to it? One reads and hears such statements every day – President Chirac of France, where I live, tells us to adapt all the time. Globalisation might as well be a force controlling our destinies just as gravity keeps our feet on the ground; a power against which mere mortals are defenceless.

Those who use this confusing, ambiguous and misleading term may simply mean that national economies are highly integrated or that goods from all over the place are spectacularly visible in our shops. So what else is new? This is hardly an original discovery. For example:

> Communications between peoples are so widespread over the entire terrestrial globe that one can virtually say that the whole world is a single city with a permanent fair where every kind of merchandise is available and anyone, without leaving home, can, through the means of money, provide for himself and enjoy everything produced by the land, by animals or by human labour. What a marvelous invention![1]

That observation dates from the mid-seventeenth century. It's easy to find similar, much older texts, not to mention archeological testimony to our human inclination to travel and to trade with each other. For example, archaeologists have uncovered evidence showing that from at least 2500 BC merchants throughout the ancient world were routinely dealing in the weights and measures of at least ten different systems. Such skills enhanced trade in valuable commodities like tin, copper, gold, silver and lapis lazuli from North Africa to India. The ancients knew a thing or two about financial globalisation as well: "Merchants could easily convert [currencies] and check they weren't being cheated. This has dramatic implications for the easing of commerce at that time," says a member of the archaeological team.[2]

High finance in modern Europe began with the fourteenth-century Italian Renaissance bankers who invented sophisticated networks, instruments of credit and means of payment. Some writers have also pointed out that the twenty-first-century world is *less* economically integrated now than it was at the height of the British Empire, if only because labour, or working-age people, as well as capital, or money, was then free to go where it liked.

Millions of poor Europeans emigrated, adding immeasurably to the populations and the wealth of the United States, Canada, Australia, Argentina and other immigrant-welcoming countries. Today, although money crosses borders at a keystroke and barriers against trade in most goods and services have never been lower, flows of people have become severely restricted. Immigrants from South to North are mostly seen as a threat or a political bombshell, not as an asset. Globalisation in this sense is nowhere near as comprehensive as it was in the nineteenth and early twentieth centuries.

The word "globalisation" sounds as though it means an economic system integrating all countries, all classes and all peoples into one harmonious whole – a kind of collective march, hand in hand, towards the Promised Land. In fact it means just the opposite: extremely unequal terms of inclusion in the world economy for countries at different levels of development and unprecedented exclusion in both the North and the South from the economic process and consequently from society. Millions of people suddenly discover they have become superfluous, unnecessary both to production and to consumption.

Whereas progressives used to rail against "exploitation," today it's almost a privilege to be exploited – at least you still have a job and a role. Although these now redundant multitudes are living all over the planet, they might as well be invisible. They have no part in globalisation because it concerns only *producers* of wealth (goods or services) and *consumers* who can afford to pay for them. Globalisation takes the best and leaves the rest.*

Governments and politicians contribute little to clarifying these issues. In France, we had a completely surreal election campaign in the spring of 2002. All the candidates were making promises and acting as if France were somehow alone in the universe, with no need to take international or even European realities into account. Except for excessive and obsessive references to crime (*l'insécurité*), the issues that most affect peoples' lives barely made it into the debates and only then because of a few smaller-party candidates.

Since we seem to be stuck with the word, however, it's helpful to put one or several adjectives in front of globalisation so that its real nature is better defined. People who are fighting against its harmful effects often speak of "corporate-led," "finance-driven" or "neo-liberal" globalisation. In the United States, some also call it "neo-conservative" globalisation.

---

* See my book *The Lugano Report: On preserving capitalism in the 21st century* for a fictional account of what will need to be done with these superfluous millions.

SOME DEFINITIONS

"Corporate-led" is an accurate description. Although huge transnational corporations (TNCs for short) operating across borders have been around for decades, they have never been so numerous, so active, so rich or so politically involved – virtually writing European Commission directives, agreements under the aegis of the World Trade Organisation and large parts of the final texts of the United Nations Conferences. Never have they invested so much abroad, nor bought up so many companies outside their home countries.

Many of them have annual sales figures far greater than the Gross National Products of most states. For example, Exxon Mobil is larger than Pakistan; General Motors than Peru or Algeria; Ford and Daimler than Nigeria or Morocco, and so on. This may seem a bit like comparing apples and oranges, but it still gives a sense of the power such firms can deploy. By 2000, the UN list of the world's top one hundred economic entities included twenty-nine mega-corporations.[3]

"Finance-driven" globalisation also fits. By the end of the 1980s, Western countries had abolished most barriers to capital movements, but with the fall of the Berlin Wall these movements accelerated even further in Southern and Eastern European countries. The development of instantaneous twenty-four-hour communications has also hugely increased the volume of financial transactions. The unlimited imagination of bankers and brokers has put a dizzying number of financial "products" like derivatives, swaps, options and futures on the market, which go well beyond the more familiar stocks and bonds.

"Neo-liberal" and "neo-conservative" are recent words, both coined as far as I know in the United States about twenty years ago. It doesn't help that they mean almost the same thing. Just to add to the confusion, the word "liberal" has done a somersault in the past couple of centuries. Two hundred years ago, liberals were the progressives. They encouraged greater democracy as well as championing equality before the law and freedom of speech and of religion. Economically they were in favour of capitalism and free trade rather than rigid state control over commerce. In the US a "liberal" is still someone at least moderately to the political Left.

The distinction between neo-conservatives and neo-liberals is one of nuance. In the American vocabulary, neo-conservatives are usually more concerned with cultural matters whereas neo-liberals are better known for their economic views. The neo-cons, as they are often called, defend so-called "family values," traditional codes of morality and religion, undeviating heterosexuality; they reject government meddling in individuals' freedom to live their lives as they please and they object to special treatment (affirmative action) for women, less privileged groups and ethnic minorities.

Neo-liberalism is an economic doctrine shared by neo-conservatives, based on open competitive markets and the "price mechanism," meaning that prices must be determined by supply and demand, not by government intervention or subsidies. Neo-liberals are against most state interventions in the economy, they are pro-free trade and anti-trade unions. They see the array of social protections afforded by the welfare state as nothing but state-organised theft and consequently they want to reduce taxes.

One of their number in the US is Mr. Grover Norquist. He heads the organisation Americans for Tax Reform and says, "We want to get government down to the size where you can drown it in the bathtub." Except, of course, for the military and the new Department of Homeland Security ...

Strict neo-liberal doctrine breaks down, however, in certain cases. Free trade is all very well, but, to cite only one example, it's OK to protect American steel producers or farmers with high tariffs or subsidies. Government rules and regulations are unwelcome, except when they are tailor-made for protecting corporate interests; taxes can be a good thing if paid by someone else; and so on.

Whatever the qualifiers used – corporate-led, finance-driven or neo-liberal – they all describe world capitalism's most recent phase which it entered roughly around 1980. From the outset, say about 500 years ago, capitalism existed as a global phenomenon. The difference today lies in its scope and the nature of its major actors: giant corporations and mega-financial institutions now have remarkable latitude to set the rules that govern everyone, especially because they also frequently control the media. They seek ever greater power to bend national and international policies to fit their needs.

Corporations, financial-market operators, and governments aligned with their interests have a set of standard "truths" everyone is expected to believe. They may claim, for example, that our retirement funds are perfectly safe invested in stock markets even when financial ruins lie scattered around us like fallen temples. They may promise more and better jobs to come, but in order to deserve them labour markets must become more "flexible" – the code word for giving up the gains of the past century concerning wages, working conditions, benefits, holidays, fair hiring and firing practices, health insurance and social protection. Unions, so they claim, are a pernicious force and working people are better off without them.

The corporate and financial worlds want to make the rules but they certainly do not want to be *seen* making them, or governing anyone. Despite their recent emphasis on corporate governance they are still primarily governed by their drive for profits.

Here's an excellent definition of globalisation from Mr. Percy Barnevik, who was often named European Businessman of the Year until he was disgraced at the last by overly greedy behaviour and forced into early retirement from ABB, a company now in deep trouble:

> I would define globalisation as the freedom for my group of companies to invest where it wants when it wants; to produce what it wants, to buy and sell where it wants and to support the fewest restrictions possible coming from labour laws or social conventions.[4]

His definition has the flavour and virtue of honesty. It takes in the Holy Trinity of freedoms which TNCs and financial managers want and need: freedom of investment, freedom of capital movements, freedom to buy and sell goods and services across borders without hindrance. And let's also get rid of those tiresome laws and standards concerning employees or the communities where we happen to have sited our activities.

Other top managers put the matter somewhat differently. Like their colleagues they want freedom, often stressing the freedom to pack up and go elsewhere. To that end, they don't want to be weighed down by anything, neither by employees, by loyalties to places nor even by property.

Contrary to classic or Marxist definitions of capitalism, what counts today is much less the ownership of the means of production than control over business *activity*. Activities can now take place almost anywhere because transportation costs are low and communications and information flows are virtually free. As the former boss of General Electric, Jack Welch, put it, "ideally, every plant you have should be on a barge." Another corporate leader says even more succinctly, "whatever it is, you're a fool if you own it."

Many of his colleagues have taken these words to heart. The UN *World Investment Report 2002* explains that

> there is a growing tendency, even for large TNCs, to ... contract out more and more functions to independent firms ... Some are even opting out of production altogether, leaving contract manufacturers to handle it while they focus on innovation and marketing.[5]

Companies used to be concerned exclusively with profits. It's not that the bottom line has become unimportant, far from it, but company PR hacks now speak above all of "shareholder value," meaning the market price of the company's stock. The firm's underlying condition becomes less important than the price its shares are supposed to be worth – and sacrifices on the altar of shareholder value include innumerable jobs, because the fewer employees the lower the costs and the higher the share price.

If you want to be formal about the definition, globalisation just means the latest stage of world capitalism and the political framework that helps it thrive. The word is ideological because it conveys the ideas that best serve the interests of people who profit from present economic, social and political arrangements. When they use the word, they want you to believe that globalisation is universal and of universal benefit. This is rubbish, but it's potent rubbish that can sometimes help to stave off popular anger and revolt.

Fortunately, both anger and revolt are on the rise.

GLOBALISED COMMUNICATIONS AND
THE INFORMATION-POOR

Sometimes when people talk about globalisation they confuse the means which allow greater economic integration – electronic communications and the internet – with the thing itself. The "web definition" of globalisation is far too narrow, but even if we use it, it's clear that only a tiny fraction of the world's population is by that standard "globalised." The World Bank used to remind us that "half the world has never made a phone call." This alarming figure may have dropped slightly, but for most human beings internet communication is even less accessible than a telephone.

The so-called "Digital Divide" echoes the divide between rich and poor in other areas. Computer use has grown prodigiously. According to sociologist Manuel Castells, there were nine million internet users in 1995, probably about 700 million in 2002, and there will be perhaps 2 billion by 2005–2007. Even with this incredible acceleration, huge disparities remain and are likely to last. No one will be surprised to learn that the best connected are also the richest – about half the population of the United States, between twenty and thirty percent in most European countries, but less than one percent in Africa or South Asia.[6]

Content providers for the internet – although they could theoretically work anywhere – are also concentrated in the great Northern urban centres because that's where the information, the high-tech gurus (and most of the fun) are. But when it comes to employment, people anywhere who lack access to the internet are now handicapped. One recent, somewhat encouraging development in wealthier Northern countries, starting with the United States, is that poorer people and minorities are beginning to have more access to electronic communications, but this is far from the case in Third World countries.

There is no doubt, however, that the communication revolution has also benefited people proposing alternatives, that technology works for them as well as for their adversaries. Even in the South, foes of neo-liberalism generally belong to organisations that have access to the internet. They can be in closer touch with each other and with their colleagues in the North than was ever before possible.

Still, whenever one uses the word globalisation, it would be well to remember that much of the world, especially the female part, doesn't know how to read and write or has no access to a pencil, paper or post office, much less a computer. This is why advocates of the Trinity of Freedoms often say things like "the problem of Africa is not too much globalisation but too little," which is true enough but not much help.

GLOBALISATION AND ME

Before we examine some of the major components and proponents of globalisation in more detail, try the experiment of looking at your own day, your own activities, even your own anxieties, from the perspective of globalisation, from the time your foreign-made alarm clock goes off in the morning until you turn off the US television sitcom and go to bed. Your clothes, your breakfast, your car, the latest fad your kids have latched onto – anything can serve as an example.

Maybe you work for a branch of a transnational company that might close down in your country and look for greener, cheaper pastures elsewhere. Maybe you are part of the public services, under intense pressure to privatise. Maybe you've put part of your savings in mutual funds or the stock market, or perhaps, like so many others, you lost part of your assets in the market plunge of the early twenty-first century.

Will your children be as well or better off than you? Will their education still be free and of high quality? Will they speak fluent English because without it ...? Will corporate control of health, schools, water, transport and everything else soon be the norm? Has the environmental crisis hit you directly through severe storms or floods?

At the end of your experiment you'll probably have your own globalisation story to tell. Here is a more general one.

THE WASHINGTON CONSENSUS

Has neo-liberal globalisation just happened? Is it some sort of historical force sweeping all before it, one which no one could foresee much less control? Hardly. It's the outcome of over two decades of specific political choices made by the most powerful actors in the world system.

The set of policies they favour is often summed up as the "Washington Consensus" because the United States is the fount of this worldview.[7] Neo-liberal doctrine, bolstered by the US government and embodied and practised by international institutions, has been relentlessly imposed throughout the world resulting in glaring disparities unworthy of, and in stark contrast to, the collective wealth and knowledge of the twenty-first century.

Imposed how? Often through the mechanism of debt. Developing countries of the South and "transition" countries (former Soviet Union Republics and satellites) with heavy debt loads have had to obey the instructions of the International Monetary Fund or face international bankruptcy. The IMF is one of the main enforcers of the Washington Consensus, which we'll just call the WC from now on. Because of debt, the IMF can act as a world policeman and give orders to supposedly sovereign states because without its seal of approval they will get no credit from any source, public or private. Other Consensus enforcers are the World Bank and the World Trade Organisation, whose policies bear a striking resemblance to those of the US Treasury.

When the various elements of WC doctrine are applied to indebted countries, they are called Structural Adjustment Programmes, or more accurately, "shock therapy." The principle aspects of the WC doctrine amount to a kind of economic and political rule-book for neo-liberal globalisation and can be summed up as follows:

1   Encourage competition in all endeavours, at all levels. People, firms, regions, and nations are in competition with each other. Survival of the fittest, devil take the hindmost, fallen by the wayside – all the clichés fit. At a time when scientists increasingly recognise the vital role of cooperation in maintaining species and natural systems, mainstream economists and businessmen have never been more primitively Darwinist or more blatantly nineteenth century in espousing the war of all against all.

  A major exception to this rule of savage competition is, however, the very largest transnational corporations which compete with each other less and less on the basis of prices. As the strong devour the weak, many sectors are becoming characterised by tight or loose informal cartels with a small number of TNCs in control.

2   Keep inflation low, that is, prevent wage–price–wage increases in an upward spiral which reduces a currency's

purchasing power. At the merest sign of inflation, jack up the country's interest rates. This will keep credit tight and dampen the money supply. The *only* mandate of the European Central Bank is to control inflation. Not a word of it concerns full employment or economic expansion. Employment is encouraged by low interest rates because they allow companies and individuals to borrow more easily, especially for big-ticket items like cars or household equipment, and thus contribute to economic activity and creating more jobs.

But sometimes economies get stuck in a trough where there's no inflation, yet there is sluggish or contracting economic activity. Many argue that interest rates in the US and Europe were reduced too little too late and that these policies are responsible for economic stagnation and job losses. The European Central Bank remains especially recalcitrant in this regard. In any case, for neo-liberal WC types, the name of the brilliant British economist John Maynard Keynes, who preached government intervention and expansionist policies, is mud.

3 Concentrate on exports and increase trade volume. Trade is by definition always good; it doesn't matter if it messes up the environment and ruins local producers. Once more, they are expected to "adapt" – whether or not they have any genuine economic alternatives – and everything will work out for the best in the end. Trade is supposed to be free as well, even though there are dozens of exceptions to this rule, many of which protect the North against exports from the South. All negotiations are geared toward making trade freer still. The Asian "tigers" like Korea, Taiwan, Singapore, Malaysia or, most successful of all, China and sometimes

India are excellent exporters. Within a matter of decades they shifted from producing low- to high-value goods and began to supply the markets of industrialised economies.

To do that, they used high tariffs to protect their infant industries against imports, and other interventionist policies which are now anathema and contrary to WC doctrine. In earlier times the now-developed nations like the United States, Great Britain, France, Germany and Japan did exactly the same thing; they all used a mix of protectionism and targeted government interventions to succeed. WC rules now allow neither. The result is that every country tends to be frozen in the place it occupied before joining the global-isation game – to the obvious benefit of those that have already reached the top of the tree and made their fortunes.

4 Allow capital to flow freely across borders, including short-term, speculative capital, even though it has been shown again and again that such movements are guaranteed even-tually to produce financial and therefore social crises. Short-term speculative capital invested in local stocks and bonds can and will leave a country in a matter of seconds whenever influential traders in New York or London feel uneasy and tap their computer keys. Hundreds of local com-panies fail, thousands of employees are thrown out of work.

During the Asian financial crisis in 1998, Malaysia and China applied controls to prevent money leaving the country. They were therefore much less affected by the crisis than their neighbours. Not being heavily indebted or under orders from the IMF, they could defy WC doctrine; but few countries are in such a position, as Mexico, Brazil, Thailand, Indonesia, Korea, Russia, Argentina and others have learned to their cost.

5 Reduce taxes on corporations and rich individuals. The doctrine claims they will then invest their tax savings and thus create jobs. More often they put their money into short-term investments (see above) or offshore tax havens (see below).

6 Do not, however, close down tax havens which many companies and rich individuals use to keep their money out of the taxman's clutches. Payment of national taxes thus falls increasingly on wage and salary earners, consumers and smaller firms, all rooted in a particular place with no access to the Cayman Islands or Monaco.* The proportion of Western governments' budgets supplied by corporations has consistently declined over the past twenty years while the share contributed by income, consumption and employment taxes has risen proportionally.

7 Privatise, privatise, privatise. A WC axiom holds that markets, left to themselves, will ensure the best economic and, therefore, the best social outcomes, nationally and internationally. Markets are efficient, governments are not. Ideally, the state should play only a distant, supervisory role, impose only the regulations businesses themselves ask for, and intervene exclusively in rare cases of market failure. Governments should have little or no part in the production of goods or services including so-called "public services."

Privatisation is the polite word for alienation or giveaways. The state enterprise that is privatised is the valuable

---

* I have it on good authority that one of the richest people in France made a deal as follows: either I pay no personal taxes or I move my company's production facilities out of France. The company is a large employer. For those above a certain level, such deals are now said to be common and governments are held hostage to this kind of blackmail.

product of years of work by hundreds or thousands of employees. Under privatisation, it is summarily handed over to wealthy individual or institutional investors. Dozens of studies, particularly concerning Great Britain, a pioneer in the field, have shown that privatisation is a failure, whatever criteria are applied – quality, price, equal access, efficiency or safety. Think of the British trains.

8 Make labour markets "flexible" and increase competition between workers. Remove protective measures for workers, like restrictions on hiring and firing; eliminate mandatory social advantages like paid holidays, health insurance, maternity/paternity leaves, "excessive" unemployment compensation or minimum wages. All these are unwanted, unjustified costs which should be done away with in the name of competition.

9 Practise "cost-recovery," i.e., fees for access to previously free services like schools and clinics, although it is well known that the consequences, particularly for girls and women, will be disastrous.

A few employers and WC types even advocate free and unlimited movement of people, because they believe, correctly as it happens, that unrestricted immigration would rapidly reduce wages and social benefits to Third World levels everywhere. They also encourage lower employment standards by lobbying governments and have usually been allowed to do so without serious opposition. But not always: major strikes and strong social movements have arisen in France, Italy and other countries to protect workers' and pensioners' rights.

WELL, DOES IT WORK?

WC supporters say that their brand of globalisation has actually improved living standards for the majority. Alternatively they may admit that perhaps much of the present generation, perhaps even the next one, may have to be sacrificed, but insist that the future, whenever that might be, is radiant.

Most people already know about the deep and growing divisions between rich and poor, both inside individual countries and between nations. They're also aware of advancing environmental degradation. Dozens of books, official reports and UN conferences have dealt with the diagnosis. Since you have presumably opened a newspaper, listened to the radio or watched television in the past twenty years or so, there's no point in even trying to summarise this work; one can merely supply a few highlights.

The first WC experiment took place in Chile. It couldn't have been carried out without the bloody, American-backed *coup d'état* against the Socialist government of Salvador Allende in 1973 (on September 11 as it happened). The generals and their economist allies, known as the "Chicago Boys" because they had taken their degrees in the most neo-liberal university economics department in the US, swept into action. General Pinochet's government murdered or "disappeared" at least three thousand people, impoverished a great many more, wiped out social safety nets and undertook the systematic destruction of the environment into the bargain.

Over the past two decades, the situation of the planet and its inhabitants has dramatically worsened; we shall deal with the ecological aspects in the following chapter. These two decades correspond roughly to the acceleration and spread of globalisation (as we'll call it from now on, with the neo-liberal, corporate-led, finance-driven qualifiers understood).

Neither the neo-liberal present nor its future is radiant, as a few courageous scholars have shown. Research at the Center for Economic and Policy Research in Washington has established that throughout the world, growth and development showed far greater gains between 1960 and 1980 than during the following twenty-year period of 1980 to 2000. They compared the two periods and found that for nearly all regions of the world, average growth rates slowed dramatically during the latter period. The exception is Asia, where growth tended to stay about the same.

Worse still, using unimpeachable methodology, the researchers found that the problem was not limited to slackening growth of the Gross Domestic Product. Improvements in child mortality, life expectancy, school enrolment and literacy, which had been quite remarkable from 1960 to 1980, all slowed to a snail's pace. Such setbacks were easily predictable, particularly since the World Bank–IMF insisted that even the poorest countries charge user fees for health and education.[8]

According to the United Nations Development Programme's (UNDP) *Human Development Report 2002*, the top five percent of the world population has an income 114 times greater than the bottom five percent. The richest ten percent of Americans alone (some 27 million people, not even one half of one percent of the world) has an income equivalent to that of the poorest forty-three percent of the world population. At the rate we're going, still according to the UNDP, it will take at least 130 years to rid the world of hunger.

At the same time, rich countries provided poor ones with an average 52 billion dollars a year (1997–2001) in "Overseas

Development Aid," or ODA, which is in free fall since the Berlin Wall tumbled and the USSR ceased to be a threat. Much of that aid also comes straight back to the donors because the money is "tied" to purchases from them.

Meanwhile, the same rich countries provide roughly one billion dollars *every day* in agricultural subsidies and support, mostly to their own largest farmers. Less than ten percent of the funds devoted worldwide to medical and biological research are available for poor peoples' diseases like malaria, tuberculosis and, increasingly, AIDS, although these scourges account for ninety percent of the global disease burden.

Although inequalities *between* countries have grown breathtakingly large, inequalities *within* countries, rich or poor, are also on the rise. Among the former, only Denmark and Canada are said by the UN to have reduced inequalities between 1979 and 1997, using the tried and true methods of taxation and redistribution (but if you ask Danes and Canadians, they dispute the official numbers). Inequalities increased most of all in the United States and the United Kingdom which have, not coincidentally, applied neo-liberal policies with the greatest enthusiasm.

INDUCED INEQUITIES

Progress towards privatisation and the wilful destruction of traditional solidarity mechanisms are unsurprisingly accompanied by spiralling inequalities. In the 1960s and 1970s the difference in remuneration between an American company president and his lowliest employee was on the order of sixty or seventy to one, already a remarkable gap. Now, however, the gap has widened to a chasm, with differences of 300 to 400 to one, depending on whose figures you use. During the Reagan decade of the 1980s, the top one percent of American families doubled their incomes, while the bottom twenty percent lost fifteen percent of the little they had.

Internal European inequalities are increasing as well, as are salary differentials, though at a slower pace and predictably more in Britain than elsewhere. European Chief Executive Officers (CEOs) are starting to demand the same salary levels, golden parachutes and stock options as their US counterparts.*

United Nations agencies have published numerous studies all concluding that disparities both within and between countries have shot up. The International Labour Organization calculates that half the world, or 3 billion people, live in poverty and that the income differential between the world's richest and poorest twenty percent has doubled over the past forty years. All the empirical evidence converges. Neo-liberal policies always have such an impact and it is indeed entirely logical that the unfettered market should reward those who have much and take from those who have little.

Mathematicians have uncovered a "power law" that has a startling number of applications in the real world: this is the 20/80 distribution pattern. When no external constraints apply, a given system will tend to evolve towards a distribution in which 20 percent of the participants obtain 80 percent of the outcomes, leaving 20 percent of the outcomes for the remaining 80 percent of the players.

Thus for income distribution, if nothing prevents it, 20 percent of the people (on earth, in a country, etc.) will hold

* Microsoft, however, abandoned stock options which created dozens of "Microsoft millionaires" in the 1990s; it will now only distribute stock shares to employees it considers deserving. The French revolted against giving Jean-Marie Messier a 20 million euro parachute for running Vivendi into the ground. Confronted with public disgust, mentalities are slowly changing in some boardrooms.

roughly 80 percent of the wealth and 80 percent of the people will share only 20 percent of the wealth. (Distribution on planet earth today is even more skewed than that). In most countries, your surname will obey a power law. If you have a common name like Smith or Williams, you are in the 80 percent who bear 20 percent of the names. If your name is more unusual, you are in the 20 percent group who share 80 percent of rarer surnames. My publisher tells me that 20 percent of the bookshops sell 80 percent of the books. 20 percent of the actors get 80 percent of the bookings, 20 percent of the banks hold 80 percent of the accounts and so on. It works in many previously unexpected areas. So if you don't want power-law wealth distribution, you have to take steps to prevent it.[9]

It is precisely because this home truth was recognised, even without sophisticated mathematics, that the European Keynesian model was developed and adopted after many social struggles. Taxation and redistribution are the key; the share of value distributed between labour and capital is one measure of success. In this distribution, according to several French economists, European labour has lost about ten points over the past two decades, with its wealth share down from about 70 to about 60 percent.

Defenders of neo-liberal policies generally claim that they are pulling people out of poverty. They cite the example of the Asian tigers. This claim is ironic, even laughable. These countries have indeed improved peoples' living standards in the past few decades, but they did so using methods in complete contradiction with neo-liberal doctrine and the WC. Unfortunately, other nations aspiring to similar achievements are no longer allowed to use these successful approaches.

INEQUALITIES ARE BAD FOR YOUR HEALTH
AND YOUR GROWTH

WC doctrine, because it fosters huge disparities, is not even in line with its supporters' pretended goal of high growth. An economist who has worked with both the United Nations University and UNICEF argues that inequality is "detrimental to growth" – not that growth is necessarily all that great either, but that is a separate discussion we will deal with later. Since growth is the Holy Grail of the WC you would think its friends would listen to economists like Giovanni Andrea Cornia.[10]

Cornia explains that in poor countries, where most land is in the hands of large landholders, you get lower agricultural production, higher food prices and you also force the poor who have little or no land to overexploit their limited environment.* Deforestation and creeping deserts are bad for everyone, creating increased global warming and population pressures.

In high-inequality countries, people are less educated and less healthy because their governments are less willing or able to tax the rich and redistribute. This in turn prevents the formation of "human capital," as economists like to call readily employable, productive people, which is low and slow. Uneducated women also have far more children than educated ones and so fuel the inequality cycle by perpetuating the ratio of lots of poor people to just a few rich ones.

This small, wealthy class wants to consume expensive imports. Freely importing lots of goodies which have to be paid for in dollars or other hard currency, they help get their

* There's the power law at work again.

country into debt. Since the country is also spending a fortune on armaments, usually paying for expensive imported oil and frequently investing in white-elephant prestige projects which supply few jobs and create no wealth, the debt mountain soon becomes overwhelming. The poor majority is then forced to sacrifice so that the government can pay the interest on its debt. This creates even more inequality.

Huge differences in wages reduce the incentive to work hard. People think "Why bother?" since they're not going to be materially rewarded anyway. The combination of poorly educated, unhealthy populations in highly indebted countries in turn reduces incentives for foreign investment, and so on.

The flip side of this coin, still according to Cornia, is "too much" equality, which is also bad for growth and living standards. Like highly unequal Third World countries, the former Socialist Republics in the Soviet bloc also had very low productivity growth. He thinks this is at least partly due to comparatively narrow differences in income. Again, people thought "Why bother?" as they had only a slim chance of greater rewards. This led to the famous syndrome "we pretend to work and they pretend to pay us." The problem for governments is to find what Cornia calls the "efficient inequality range" and then make policy to stay within that range, nobody left out, but nobody making obscene amounts of money either and lording it over everyone else.

The least one can say is that ardent globalisers have not given houseroom to the policies Cornia recommends. With the advent of the Thatcher–Reagan tandem (UK 1979, US 1981), neo-liberal globalisation took its great leap forward. Greed was good. A decade later, the fall of the Berlin Wall followed by the disintegration of the Soviet Union eliminated the world's only competing economic system and allowed the WC to once more hugely broaden its scope.*

The consequences have been severe.

MASSAGING THE FIGURES

The World Bank has tried to prove that the number of people worldwide living in "absolute poverty" has been steadily falling, thanks to WC policies, which are thus supposed to be "working" or "on the right track." The Bank's annual *World Development Report* is the usual source for figures on poverty and, since the Bank has the biggest specialised research shop on the planet, nearly everyone takes whatever the Bank says at face value.

But not everyone. For example, two professors at Columbia University, Sanjay Reddy and Thomas Pogge, have produced a long paper pointedly titled "How *Not* to Count the Poor." They pretty much demolish the Bank's statistics as well as the methodology and assumptions those statistics are based on. The reader ends up agreeing with them that "the Bank's estimates of the level, distribution and trend of global poverty should not be accepted," that the Bank is in fact guilty of a "substantial underestimation of the extent of world poverty."[11]

The Bank neglects several factors crucial to determining the numbers of the poor worldwide. It's particularly weak on India and China (a mere one-third of humanity) and it assumes that

* Please do not mistake my meaning. I was never a fan of the State Socialist system but it did provide societies with a bulwark against the neo-liberal onslaught, not just in Eastern Europe but frequently in the South as well. Ten years after its demise, the poverty rate in Russia has been multiplied by thirty and male life expectancy has been reduced by seven years.

growth automatically benefits the poor, without bothering to look at how that growth is actually distributed among the population. But Reddy and Pogge uncover other serious flaws.

First, the nature and the variety of goods consumed by the poor differ markedly from those consumed by the general population. Furthermore, for all kinds of reasons, the poor generally have to pay more than those better off for the same goods. Finally, the disproportionate amount of the most basic foodstuffs like bread, rice or other cereals in their diets, and the local prices for these vital goods, take a big bite from incomes that are borderline to begin with.

If all the methodological gaps and errors (and many others too technical to examine here) were taken into account, the Bank's calculations of the numbers of poor people would have to be dramatically revised: depending on the country, the poverty headcount would jump by anywhere between one third and sixty percent. Instead of "only" 1.3 billion people living in "absolute poverty," which in Bank-speak is different from and far worse than just plain poverty, there may well be over 2 billion, approximately one-third of the world's population.

It seems fair to say that the Washington Consensus definitely does not work, at least not for the people who are most at risk. Nor does it work for the planet, whose state we'll look at next before returning to the major actors on the globalised stage.

2

... WE SALVAGE THE PLANET

ECONOMY AND ECOLOGY

Just as corporations care nothing about human beings or societies per se, so they are indifferent to nature when it is not directly useful to them in terms of profit or reputation.

But beyond that, I want to argue that capitalism and environmental sustainability, as it is now fashionably called, are logically and conceptually incompatible. Two worldviews, the ecological and the economic, are locked in warfare, whether or not this war has yet been generally recognised. The outcome of this war will decide nothing less than the future of humanity and indeed whether or not humanity even *has* a future.

Sorry to sound so apocalyptic; but the fact remains that the contradictions between economy and ecology are so deep that we ignore them at our peril. Despite the "turtles and Teamsters, united at last" in Seattle, I fear that much of the global justice movement has not yet integrated the natural environment into its analysis and action.* In this respect, alas, it's

---

* At the 1999 protests against the World Trade Organisation in Seattle, environmentalists in turtle costumes (to remind the WTO of its decision to allow fishing boats without Turtle Excluder Devices to continue decimating sea turtles) marched side by side with the Teamsters (the truck-drivers union) and many other trade unions, an impossible alliance in earlier years.

not much better than its adversaries.

The "eco" in economy and ecology refers to the same Greek root, *oikos*, the household, estate or domain. The eco-*nomos* is the rule, or the set of rules, for managing the domain. The eco-*logos* is the underlying principle, the spirit, the reason for it all – in the sense that Saint John affirms at the outset of his Gospel, "In the beginning was the Logos," usually translated as the "Word." Humans, animals, plants; the land and water that surround them; and their interactions, are all part of the same physical reality, the same domain.

Given the Greek root, you would think that the Logos would be seen as the greater of the two and supersede the Nomos. Normally the spirit and underlying principle should override and define the rules and regulations, so that the eco-logos would be the guiding force behind the economy.

Not so with the globalised capitalist economy which dictates the rules to society. Market forces shape most of our relationships with each other and with the natural world. The eco-nomos, the globalised economy, the marketplace, refuses to take second place to the Logos or to anything else. The Nomos has claimed planetary authority.

DANGER SIGNALS

Just as most people are already aware of the economic horrors of globalisation, so they are familiar with the catalogue of environmental hazards: global warming and climate change; disappearing ozone; razed forests; massive species extinctions; polluted air and water; disfigured coastlines; desertified, saline or paved-over land – the list goes on.

The Mediterranean sea, where European civilisation begins, is a good example. Looking at the Mediterranean today is pretty depressing. Along its 46.000 kilometres of coastline live 130 million permanent residents joined each year by at least 100 million tourists. The Mediterranean hosts fully a third of all world tourism. These populations produce an annual 500 million tons of sewage, in some places still piped untreated directly into the sea. Progress made in waste treatment over the past decade has tended to be outstripped by population increases in the southern and eastern Mediterranean. Add annually 60.000 tonnes of detergents, several thousand tonnes of heavy metals, huge quantities of nitrates from fertiliser, and at least 600.000 tonnes of petroleum from land run-offs and oil tankers emptying their residues at sea, and one begins to see the whole dirty picture.

The predatory plant *caulerpa taxifolia* escaped in the early 1980s from an aquarium in Monaco and is rapidly colonising the sea floor (easily 15.000 hectares to date), creating possibly irreversible biological pollution. Even a fragment of the plant carried on an anchor or fishing gear can form a new colony. Over-fishing and disease are destroying stocks of fish and other marine species. Dolphins are choking on plastics. Fishermen are killing off monk seals because they compete for the fish. The sea is barely flushed: the waters of the Nile are now entirely used for irrigation, Gibraltar lets virtually nothing from the Atlantic past the pillars and the Black Sea is, if anything, more polluted than the Mediterranean itself.

Such is the environmental state of the sea which has inspired poets and artists from Homer and the Minoans onwards, but for the economy it reflects excellent news. Mass tourism contributes to GNP; production of chemicals, plastics and detergents provides employment; nitrates and irrigation help boost crop yields for farmers; petroleum keeps our industries ticking over.

If you're still depressed by the state of the Mediterranean, you can go out to dinner at a nice fish restaurant, at least as long as supplies last. So never mind. A great deal of money is being made and when we've put enough aside we can afford to worry about the environment. But not just yet.

Naturally it's not only the Mediterranean or Western Europe. State Socialism caused environmental devastation on an even greater scale. The centrally planned economies of Eastern Europe were ecological disaster zones and largely remain so. They were imitating predatory Western productivist patterns that began with the Industrial Revolution and so-called "modernised" agriculture, but with even worse results because in the former Soviet Empire, citizens could not protest or organise to protect the environment.

DEREGULATION OR CORPORATE RE-REGULATION?

The eco-nomos is today triumphant and is forcibly integrating the globe according to the neo-liberal rules of the marketplace. Besides privatisation and competition, another big word in the globalisation vocabulary is "deregulation." Neo-liberal economists like this word by which they mean that states are getting rid of laws and regulations that protect their natural environments from external threats.

Like "globalisation" itself, the word "deregulation" is a trap. Plenty of rules are still in place and more are being made every day; it's just that they tend to favour the needs of capital and transnational corporations, not the planet's need to restore itself. Catastrophic oil spills like the wrecks of the *Erika* and the *Prestige* which polluted huge stretches of the Atlantic coastline in France and Spain have led to some regulatory changes, but skeptics say these are not nearly enough to prevent more marine and coastal disasters.

Nor can so-called "codes of conduct" stave off future spills. What company president proclaims, for example, that "No economic priority can stand if it is detrimental to worker safety or respect for the environment"? Thierry Desmarest, CEO of the oil giant TotalFinaElf, did so in his safety and environment charter. Yet the broken-down tub *Erika* was transporting TotalFina oil, despite another of the Charter's pronouncements: "The Group chooses its industrial and commercial partners on the basis of their capacity to respect Total's rules with regard to safety and the environment."[12]

Just as corporations can't be trusted to put genuine ecological constraints in place, so governments beholden to corporate interests will naturally fight in their corner. Deregulation in practice means, for example, that in the United States the Bush administration is dismantling environmental controls at all levels. Bush's Secretary of the Environment resigned because she could accomplish nothing.

In Europe, environmental measures are also under direct attack from the forces of globalisation. In France it took about six months for the new right-wing government to obliterate virtually all the environmental legislation passed in the previous five years, however timid and inadequate that legislation was to begin with. Farmer-activist José Bové took huge risks to warn against the dangers of genetically manipulated crops and got sentenced to prison for his pains, despite the announcement that the Precautionary Principle would henceforth be enshrined in the French constitution.

With all its annexes, the document establishing the World Trade Organisation is some twenty thousand pages long. It describes in minute detail the rights of corporations to produce, buy, sell or invest, including the right to patent life forms, across national boundaries. It contains no rules at all concerning the obligations of these same corporations to reduce waste, pollution and environmental destruction (or for that matter to pay decent wages, give workers enough time off and provide safe working conditions).

The 1992 United Nations Rio Conference was called in the name of "sustainable development." The agenda, however, was quietly shaped by transnational corporations duly grouped under the banner of the Business Council for Sustainable Development – a tragically ironic name, given that its membership included some of the world's major corporate polluters and environmental plunderers. The Business Council's great victory in Rio was to avoid all mention of regulation for corporate activity. These companies are now officially assumed to be capable of regulating themselves and they have since named their lobby the *World* Business Council for Sustainable Development and added a lot more members.

The Rio Declaration recognised that "states have the sovereign right to exploit their own resources." In reality, it's the corporations authorised to act within the boundaries of those states that have the "right to exploit" those resources and to use those environments. Countries compete to attract transnational investment. Those demanding the lowest environmental or social standards, while offering docile, ill-paid yet productive labour forces, are most likely to win the prize. No wonder China occupies the top rung of the foreign investment ladder, having attracted more than 270 billion dollars in Foreign Direct Investment since 1997.

The logic of the untrammeled market is to expand until everything – goods, services, nature itself – falls within its purview and can be freely bought and sold. The environment, in the capitalist view, is real estate and a potential building site, a source of raw materials and a place to dump wastes. One of the *New Yorker* cartoons by William Hamilton, the great satirist of the American corporate class, shows two executives looking out the window of their company jet at the earth below – "How little we really own, Tom, when you think of all there is to own," says one.

Just as the State Socialist economies behaved as badly if not worse than the capitalist ones, so both the Chinese and the Indians seem hell-bent on entering the twenty-first century via the nineteenth. They *want* to imitate the stupid development path chosen by the West instead of leapfrogging over our destructive practices straight into the twenty-first century.

It is naive to expect corporations to respect the environment unless: 1) it is profitable to do so, 2) it is legally mandated without loopholes, or 3) their reputations will suffer grave damage if they do not. The corporate imperative is to maintain and improve market share and profit in a business arena where no one is doing anyone any favours.

In order to survive, even the largest companies *must* try to ensure that someone else pays the bill for human and natural deterioration. Economists call this "externalising the costs of production." Someone beyond the company pays them or nature itself pays. Firms are dead set against internalising these costs, explaining that they would then have to charge more for their products, consumers would consume less, economic activity would contract, firms would fail and greater unemployment would result. (This reasoning is false when the rules are the same for all, but in a neo-liberal world they seldom are.)

One can hold out a modest hope, since some environmental thinkers and economists are demonstrating that the most ecologically careful production is also the most efficient and therefore most profitable, but this message is slow to take hold. We will suggest some more radical measures later on.

In a globalised system of competition for a place in the sun and a share of the market, the logic of the eco-nomos is necessarily to minimise ecological protection, to strip resources and to dump waste as cheaply as possible. This is one reason why the Nomos and Logos worldviews are antagonistic. There are other reasons as well.

WHO DECIDES, WHO PAYS?

It's true that the market can be formidably, ruthlessly efficient and do many things well. But it should not be allowed to make social and environmental choices in our stead. Through democratic debate, society has to set limits on the market, determine what goods and services should or should not be bought and sold in the marketplace and decide who pays the costs now externalised. These are political questions in the deepest sense because they touch upon the power to dictate the circumstances of everyone's life.

The real debate of our time, which almost never takes place, should concern these limits and, above all, who has the power to make the rules. Despite repeated disasters, most economists still claim we should simply let the market get on with its business since it is the best allocator of resources whether they be natural, man-made or human. Ultimately, they say, it will also recognise and outlaw waste and ecological destruction by making them too costly.

Neo-liberal theorists often point to Adam Smith, the great eighteenth-century founder of liberalism, who proclaimed that millions of people pursuing their own self-interest in the marketplace would lead to unintended but benign social outcomes.

They now add that the market, left to itself, can also lead to benign environmental outcomes.

Poor Adam Smith! He never thought of himself as an economist but as a moral philosopher. He saw man as a social being, possessed of what he called "fellow feeling," deeply concerned with the good opinion of others. Although he was the first theorist of competition, Smith was convinced that in the competitive race a man will not "jostle or throw down any of his competitors" because he is too mindful of the "spectator" who is observing and judging his behaviour. In modern terms, he would be worried about public opinion. In the twenty-first-century globalised world, by contrast, everyone tries to jostle and throw down any competitor who might threaten market share and profits; and for neo-liberals, who refer to Adam Smith all the time, this is perfectly normal.[13]

Smith's reasoning about self-interest leading to benign outcomes may have been adequate for small-island Britain in 1776, but he was wrong about human behaviour and social outcomes in a globalised, competitive world space. In particular, the famous "Invisible Hand" and capitalist market self-regulation do not and cannot work in the case of *ecological* outcomes. As Garret Hardin showed decades ago in his famous and influential article "The Tragedy of the Commons," a competitive environment requires that each fisherman or logger catch as many fish or cut down as many trees as he can, right now. Each individual pursuing self-interest will be devastating to the interests of nature.[14]

Hardin failed to recognise that in the case of cooperative property management, the "commons" – whether English pastures, Cameroonian forests or Maine lobster fisheries – can be sustained indefinitely. Such an outcome requires, however, that only the members of the concerned group be able to make the rules and decide who is a member of their group and who isn't. Social pressure from the group then prevents any one member from trying to extract more than his share. Successful management of the commons hinges less on public-versus-private than on group-versus-individual ownership. It is capitalist individualism that pits each against all, forces everyone to maximise gains in the short term, and ruins common property resources.[15]

The picture is the same for firms. In a capitalist economy, each oil or chemical company has an interest to clean its tanks or dispose of its wastes efficiently, if necessary in the Mediterranean if that's the cheapest solution (and unless it's afraid of getting caught breaking the law and damaging its reputation). It is in each individual farmer's interest to apply fertiliser; never mind the run-offs. Business schools actually teach students to measure the advantages of breaking the law and the probability of getting caught against the costs of behaving legally.

FREE RIDES

A few years ago I had the luck to visit the Ionian coast of Turkey. The frenetic pace of hotel and high-rise apartment construction there vastly outstripped local capacity to keep the sea or the beaches clean, because to do so would necessarily be a collective undertaking whether public or private. Environmental protection is by necessity collective and must be accompanied by enforceable rules.

Otherwise, the well-known paradox of the free rider immediately surfaces: anyone volunteering to start the clean-up single-handedly is, economically speaking, a fool because he will pay the costs, yet allow everyone else to reap the benefits.

If no collective authority, stemming either from the local community, an authoritative business association or the state, specifically decides to clean up after the mess of raw capitalist entrepreneurship, or forces the entrepreneurs to do so themselves, the environment, and public health, will suffer.

When capital can cross borders at will and seek out new places to set up factories, strip resources, exploit cheap labour and dump wastes, it is naturally hostile to regulation. This is not a moral judgment, merely the nature of the beast. Let's assume, however, for the sake of argument that nearly everyone recognises the need for international regulation. Even then, for the system to work, all corporations and all countries, rich and poor, would have to adopt the same standards at virtually the same time. Otherwise, the first countries or companies to take the initiative of *internalising* ecological costs would be the fools, putting themselves at an immediate economic disadvantage. They might gain in the long run, but capitalism rarely offers a run that long.

We do not have incentive systems to reward countries and companies that play fair and look beyond short-term interests. Some companies claim they do so anyway. If these claims can be independently verified, they should be saluted and where possible the companies concerned should be helped to overcome the cost disadvantage their decent behaviour can entail, especially at the beginning.

CAPITALIST SPACE, CAPITALIST TIME

Just as capitalist nature is nothing but a source of raw materials and a site for waste dumping, so the market functions within a time framework contrary to the reality of natural time. Production (of goods) and re-production (of species or natural systems) are different processes and do not obey the same temporal rules. Nature cannot be hurried; it requires rest and renewal. Nature's rhythms contrast sharply with the speed of the marketplace which is a creature of the eternal present, always focused on that imaginary point where supply intersects with demand and price is established. And in the marketplace, the fast devour the slow.

Market actors must try their best to compress natural time. The first step to achieve faster production is often to eliminate human beings from the process, but when that proves impossible or undesirable one can find ways to make the labour force move faster. Ever since the Industrial Revolution and Taylorism (workers on assembly lines making the same robotic, "efficient" gestures every day) a major source of friction between labour and management has been production speed-ups. To make their female workforce go faster, the owners of one plant in Thailand put amphetamines in the drinking water; some of the workers later gave birth to deformed babies. The market wants plants to grow faster and animals to mature faster. No wonder we're losing biodiversity and raising herds of mad cows.

Philosophically speaking, the opposition between economic time and natural time is epistemological – a basic conflict between ways of seeing and explaining the world. The keywords here are *reversible* and *irreversible*. Since the time of Adam Smith, standard economics textbooks have treated economic processes as inherently reversible. They always assume that endless permutations are possible, backwards, forwards and sideways; permutations between land, labour and capital; between investment, rent, wages, profits and other supposedly independent variables. Economists, including Marxist ones, love such processes because they are so much simpler to deal with. All of them are supposed to be capable of reverting to "initial conditions."

Sad to say, nature doesn't function according to the laws of Newtonian mechanics. Natural systems do not revert to initial conditions. On the contrary, the serious changes they undergo are usually permanent and irreversible at least within our poor human timescale. Once a tropical forest is cut down, experts say it would need a minimum of 400 years to regenerate and even then one could not be sure of the result.

I am writing in 2003 during one of the hottest – if not *the* hottest – European summers on record. People can talk of nothing else. On the news bulletin this morning announcing a new day of record temperatures was the terrible story of a nine-year-old child chained to his bed and beaten to death by his family. The parents, the uncle and grandmother were immediately arrested because *they were responsible.*

During the heatwave, deaths in France have reached epidemic proportions: statistically an extra ten thousand people have been wiped out. The hospitals are overflowing, nuclear reactors risk overheating, fires are raging, crops are grilled in the fields. Yet no one is responsible. One wonders what it will take to force people and especially governments to reduce greenhouse gas emissions right now. We need no further proof that it's our own human activities that have led to higher temperatures and more frequent storms of unprecedented violence.

Why don't we apply the full force of the law to those responsible for global warming? They can be identified. We must overhaul the fossil-fuel economy, the building codes, the transport industry. Individuals alone can't do it even if we all behave with the greatest ecological responsibility, because in this case "we" are responsible for less than a quarter of greenhouse gas emissions. Intellectually we know all we need to know, technologically we could remedy our plight starting today, but inertia and vested interests rule. Sorry, but I can't help venting as well as sweating. It's because I'm scared – for my children, my grandchildren and everyone else's, for civilisation, for life.*

Perhaps nothing short of a large-scale catastrophe will suffice, at which point it may well be too late. Although I hope I am wrong, I fear action may be impossible not just because of the interests that oppose it, but as a matter of pure logic. Global warming has already produced incalculable economic effects but neo-classical economics can't deal with its causes. The economic indicators on which we rely are unable to predict disaster. The market will never warn us of impending ecological catastrophe until it is too late. This is nonetheless what we inherently ask and expect it to do.

Because we have become so accustomed to relying on market signals, especially changes in prices, for virtually all our economic and political decisions, we fail to recognise that in the crucial area of environmental decline and breakdown, the market is going to be deathly silent. We continue to apply static, mechanical, reversible methodologies to natural phenomena which are governed instead by dynamic, chaotic and irreversible forces. Here's another illustration:

Take the orthodox market view in which extra units of anything – let's say CO_2 – added to the biosphere at uniform rates will give $1+1+1$, etc., and make a nice straight oblique line on the graph as $1+1+1$, etc., can be expected to do. On this ideal

---

* But as I correct the proofs in a cooler moment, let me add that Britain, like Germany and Denmark, seems to have recognised the advantages of wind power not just for reducing greenhouse gases but for job creation and export opportunities.

graph, this process can theoretically continue forever. In nature, however, the addition of an extra unit of CO_2 can become *at any time* the straw that breaks the camel's back and makes the curve fly off the chart. The market will never give you advance warning. It will only send you the signal of "too much" when it is too late.

The natural environment is not subject to our crude elementary math but rather to complex feedback loops, sharp shifts, and comparatively sudden systemic collapse and reorganisation. A few isolated economists are beginning to listen to scientists like Per Bak who has shown how large, complex, interactive systems organise themselves to a critical state in which an unpredictable, minor event sparks a chain reaction that can lead to a breakdown. Bak calls this state "self-organised criticality." The chain reaction is sometimes also known as the sand pile effect in which the final pinch of sand makes all the difference.

Market prices rarely even tell us about scarcity, the bedrock upon which standard economics stands. Scarcity means something can be bought and sold; if an item isn't scarce, it has no price and therefore no market, end of story. So far, no one has managed to sell air, although the idea of a market for "pollution rights permits" comes fairly close.

Theoretically, the scarcer the commodity, the higher the price. Note, however, that a great many poorer Southern players are competing for export revenues and are exporting the same small range of primary products. The flood of exports means prices are low, no matter how scarce the resource may actually be. So long as supplies last, the market is completely insensitive to the depletion of natural capital, like fish, forests and soil. No matter how rare a good may become in absolute terms, exports will continue as long as there is anything physically left to export. Prices will not tell us about the true level of stocks or the fragility of the natural systems we depend on.

Depredation is costly. Argentina is in the midst of a long-term, debilitating and socially disastrous financial crisis. The country's debts are staggering and it must export whatever comes to hand to earn the money to pay interest. The head of the UN Environment Programme says that Argentina has multiplied its fish catch by five since 1985 and fish firms have earned an estimated 1.6 billion dollars. Great news? No, because according to UNEP, the depletion of fish stocks has led to net *costs* of about 500 million dollars in terms of damage to fish populations.

Mainstream economists find views like mine alarmist. Not only do most of them deny natural limits but they also believe that the market can solve all human problems, including ecological problems. Take, for example, the opinion of Mr. Larry Summers who was Chief Economist at the World Bank and later Under-Secretary of the US Treasury in charge of International Affairs. He is now President of Harvard, the oldest and probably most prestigious university in the United States, but this doesn't change the fact that he is ecologically illiterate. Summers is best known for his leaked statement that Africa was "seriously under-polluted" and should be paid for importing toxic wastes from elsewhere – he later said he was not being literal but exaggerating on purpose to make a point. The following anti-ecological statement can't escape criticism on those grounds:

> There are no ... limits to the carrying capacity of the earth that are likely to bind at any time in the foreseeable future. There isn't a risk of an apocalypse due to global warming or anything else. The idea that the world is headed over an abyss is profoundly wrong. The idea

that we should put limits on growth because of some natural limit is a profound error and one that, were it ever to prove influential, would have staggering social costs.[16]

Summers's logic is echoed by British economist, World Bank consultant and Emeritus Fellow of Balliol College, Oxford, Wilfred Beckerman in his anti-environmentalist tract titled *Small is Stupid: Blowing the Whistle on the Greens*. Beckerman accuses ecologists of fabricating "melodramatic disaster scenarios." Like other mainstream economists, including Summers, he claims that the answer to environmental problems is more economic growth.[17]

The richer we become, the theory goes, the more funds we can devote to environmental repair and clean-up. Even if we don't have the necessary technology now, future generations will come up with it. Besides, according to Beckerman, economic growth is itself responsible for greater environmental awareness. It is "economic growth that has allowed a shift in people's priorities from the satisfaction of basic needs to a concern with their environment and a greater willingness to devote resources to environmental protection." This was also the principle message promoted by business at the Rio Conference on Sustainable Development in 1992.

WHICH SYSTEM RULES?

Summers and Beckerman are perfect illustrations of a worldview which sees the economy as the total system, with everything else, including nature, subordinate to it. Look out the window: that's about all it takes to recognise that the manmade economy operates within the confines of the natural world of which human beings are only a part.

This is so simple and obvious that it is almost always over-looked. A far more realistic and sane way of looking at the global economy does exist.* Unfortunately, it has yet to penetrate the calculations of economists and the projects of politicians.

Imagine a cube which represents the economy. It is set inside the biosphere, a large but finite sphere. In this vision, the productive process is embedded in nature. The sphere is necessarily closed because even if we husband our resources and control our pollution and wastes more intelligently, we cannot increase the given capacity of the biosphere no matter what our present or future technology.

The man-made economy "imports" high-grade energy and matter from the biosphere (this is the biosphere's "source" function), uses them in production and then "exports" its wastes and used-up energy (heat) into the biosphere (this is the "sink" function). Nature can only provide and assimilate so much; its capacity both as a source and as a sink is limited. Most important of all, no matter what we do, we can never put the sphere inside the cube.

This alternative vision of economics is based on the laws of thermodynamics, on flows of matter and energy and the creation of waste and useless heat, or entropy. Once you begin thinking in this way, the arguments seem blindingly, inescapably true, but it's incredibly difficult to convince the economics profession of those truths.

Anyone familiar with systems analysis will confirm that the rules of a subsystem do not govern the rules of the total system. This may be why it seems so hard to get economists,

* This vision was pioneered by Nicholas Georgescu-Roegen in the early 1970s and has since been popularised by ecological economists like Herman Daly or in France René Passet.

with a few notable and honourable exceptions, to draw the circle of the biosphere around the square of the economy. They would then have to admit that the biosphere is the total system and economy only an increasingly predatory subsystem.

This observation has huge practical consequences. One is that questions of scale become crucial. If the cube of the economy is small in proportion to the total capacity of the biosphere, as it was in the eighteenth or nineteenth century, no problem. Today, however, we are producing in less than two weeks the entire global output of the year 1900. At present rates, the scale of the world economy doubles in less than twenty-five years.

Some biologists have estimated that humans are already appropriating for their own use roughly forty percent of what they call the Net Primary Product or Net Photosynthetic Product (NPP), basically everything the energy of the sun now produces or has produced. The NPP measures the impact of human use of food, fuel, fibre and other plant output, plus human destruction of ecosystem potential through deforestation, over-fishing, desertification and the like. This human appropriation of NPP is also calculated to double roughly every twenty-five years. If these figures are exact – the scientific article giving the details was published in 1986 and another confirmed them in 2001 – then at present rates we shall reach eighty percent human appropriation of NPP before the year 2015 and 160 percent appropriation before 2040, by which time we shall have already kissed the planet goodbye.[18]

Furthermore, work undertaken by William Rees and Mathis Wackernagle at the University of Vancouver in Canada suggests that the richest billion and a half people in the world are appropriating, right now, for their exclusive use, *the entire biophysical output of the planet*. What Larry Summers wrongly calls "global carrying capacity" is already hugely overshot. Under these circumstances, natural degradation can only increase exponentially.

The Vancouver team calls this phenomenon the "ecological footprint," a novel unit measuring human impact on the biosphere according to income. In this vision, nature must not merely accommodate more people, but also *larger* people. Rich people "weigh" more and take up more space because they consume so much more than poor ones.[19]

Here is Rees's definition of his unit of measure:

> The ecological footprint is the corresponding area of productive land and aquatic ecosystems required to produce the resources used, and to assimilate the *wastes* produced, by a defined population at a specified material standard of living, wherever on Earth that land may be located. (his emphasis)

Using the same method, ecologist Herbert Girardet has calculated that London, with twelve percent of the British population, has a footprint 125 times larger than its own size and requires to sustain it the equivalent of all the productive land in the UK. Rees's own home city of Vancouver, needs 174 times its own area; Holland needs five to seven times its own surface area, and so on.[20] With 10 or 11 billion people on earth, if population growth continues at present rates, we'll need five or six extra planets, even assuming no further environmental degradation takes place.

GROWTH AND LOGICAL IMPOSSIBILITIES

Even if the figures put forward by these biologists and ecologists are way off, they still illustrate the ecological dilemma we face. Humans rely on other species; we can't simply grab the entire Net Photosynthetic Product and leave nothing for other living creatures, if only because it would be suicidal. Besides, the NPP isn't going to grow significantly even with improved technology. It is not under the control of the Davos World Economic Forum, Bill Gates, or anyone else. For the first time in history, humans face not just a natural impossibility but a mathematical, logical one as well, and they can't seem to accept that fact.

Since it believes that continual growth holds the solution to all our problems it's no wonder the economics profession balks at and rejects the ecological worldview. But as the late ecological economist Kenneth Boulding reminded us, "when something grows, it gets bigger." Growth is not the solution but the problem. For most economists, this is the ultimate heresy, too shocking even to be contemplated or discussed. Denial of physical and biological reality can become a way of thinking and a way of life.

Some economists try to escape the dilemma by claiming that man-made capital can substitute for natural capital. We need to invest and improve our technology to the point that it won't matter how much natural capital we strip from the planet. This is another specious argument. Most man-made capital is still directly dependent on underlying natural resources. To use one of Herman Daly's examples, it makes no difference how many sawmills you have if there are no more trees; nor how many trawlers and canneries when there are no more fish. As for the sink functions of nature, like dumping CO_2 into the atmosphere, what man-made capital can save us from the consequences of severe climate change?

What if we were to embrace the alternative logic, the unconventional vision of the ecological economists, and recognise that nature is the total system and our man-made economy is only a subsystem subject to its rules? Would this mean the end of the good life? Surely not. In fact, we have everything to gain from an unromantic, realistic vision of the biosphere as the total system and the economy as the subsystem, not only because our lives and future depend on it but also because those lives would actually be better.

Practically speaking, if we accept alternative premises and a changed vision, the first question is how much bigger *can* the economy get and second, how much bigger *should* it get? It clearly can't go on doubling every twenty-five years. This is all to the good. Much of what we call growth is nothing more than the destruction of natural capital counted as income.

Furthermore, much so-called "growth" is making us poorer or is vainly trying to compensate for past economic and social failures. Prison construction, reconstructive surgery, cancer treatments, anti-theft devices in automobiles, reconstruction after terrorist attacks and wars are all contributing to growth. It would be absurd to conclude that more prisoners, thefts, cancers and so on are desirable.

Economic growth, it is true, once correlated quite closely with increases in overall welfare, but this has ceased to be the case for at least a couple of decades. More and more growth is related to phenomena most people would rather do without. Steps to clean up a fouled environment will surely rank high on the list of growth-inducing projects in the coming years. Why not simply keep it clean to begin with? Overall welfare would increase even if growth did not.

Our statisticians don't even know how (or if they do, aren't allowed) to measure the proportion of present growth which is the result of trying to make up for past negligence; our national accounts do not distinguish between genuine, positive,

wealth- and welfare-producing growth and growth that impov-
erishes us. To my knowledge, only the Norwegians and the
Dutch have seriously tried, conceptually speaking, to determine
which is which. In France, Patrick Viveret is doing pioneering
work on what constitutes genuine wealth and how to measure
it. But for the most part, we are trying to understand our highly
complex economies with extraordinarily crude tools.[21]

ANOTHER ENVIRONMENT IS POSSIBLE

How might we become more sophisticated or at least less
primitive in our worldview? Mere awareness of ecological
problems, even if widespread, will never suffice to guarantee
changes in policy. "Consciousness raising" is no substitute for
building new *rapports de force*, new balances of power. To bring
about change we shall have to confront not just inertia and
indifference even within the global justice movement but also
many entrenched interests which for reasons already noted will
put their own short-term gains first. We will return to this
problem later.

In 2002, the World Summit on Sustainable Development
met in Johannesburg a decade after the first environmental
summit (not counting the pioneering Stockholm conference in
1972) in Rio. The Jo'burg summit was supposed to deal with
both the environment and poverty but, just as the progressive
camp feared, it was a dismal failure with the Americans
blocking every possible advance.

We cannot pull everyone on earth out of poverty and
provide all human beings with a decent standard of living
unless the official "developers" immediately switch to clean
energy and clean production. As both China and India show,
the South will not take this path spontaneously because, for the

moment, it is more expensive. If China and India – 2 billion people – continue on the fossil-fuels road, as they show every sign of doing, permanent and undoubtedly devastating climate alteration is a certainty. This is the vicious circle only public spending can break.

In the North, we need desperately to change our production methods, although this may be just as hard as challenging consumption habits. It is nonetheless possible to shift to an economy embedded in the natural environment without renouncing the good life. Work done in Germany at the Wuppertal Institute by Ernst-Ulrich von Weiszächer, translated into English as *Factor Four: Doubling Wealth, Halving Resource Use* contains numerous examples of ways to maintain or improve standards of living while weighing more lightly on the earth.*

The eco-nomos, capitalist market approach to globalisation through competition and the war of all against all can only lead to collective disaster. The opposite view, that of the eco-logos, makes cooperation between people, and between people and nature, central to our choices. The reductionist view, with its primitive Darwinism, is, thank God, being challenged. More and more people recognise that human success is not based on the "survival of the fittest." We first became capable of creating an economic surplus, and the culture and art that accompanied it, through cooperation and collaboration.

To end on a slightly Zen note, if you are in Oxford and you want to go to London but find yourself on the road to Manchester the answer is not to go faster and faster towards Manchester but to stop, turn around, and head for London.

---

* Von Weiszächer actually wanted to call his book "Factor Ten" because he believes ecological methods could reduce our impact on the earth by that much – but his publishers thought that was too extreme.

3

... WE IDENTIFY THE ACTORS

Here we turn to the major globalisation actors in both the public and private sectors. We already have a passing acquaintance with some of them and will meet them again shortly in their role as adversaries.

PUBLIC ACTORS

1 The Terrible Twins: the World Bank and the International Monetary Fund

Compared to their size, complexity and influence, the Bank and the Fund will get regrettably little space here. For example, in 1995 I co-authored a whole book about the World Bank,[22] and the IMF is not merely debtmeister to the universe but has many other strings to its bow.

The Terrible Twins were born at the famous conference in Bretton Woods, New Hampshire, in 1944. The plans for their establishment were conceived by British economist John Maynard Keynes and his American counterpart Harry Dexter White. This is why the Bank and Fund are sometimes called "the Bretton Woods institutions" (BWI) or "Keynes's twins." They did not seem in the least terrible then.

Both were in fact progressive institutions for the time. The Bank, whose formal name is the "International Bank for Reconstruction and Development" was founded to put war-torn Europe back on its feet ASAP. It made loans for the reconstruction of war-ravaged European infrastructure, but Keynes was thinking of the post-colonial as well as the post-war world and that is where the "Development" in its title comes in.

The Fund was supposed to make loans to countries with temporary "balance of payments" problems, that is, when there was no more money in the till and they risked dropping out of the world trading system. Neither institution was supposed to function as an arbiter of internal national policies nor make their loans conditional on following certain policy prescriptions.

The money came from contributions made almost entirely by the rich countries. Voting strength on the basis of "one dollar one vote" reflected this imbalance. For example, the United States has enough shares to block any major decision at the Fund which requires an eighty-five percent majority.

Both the IMF and the Bank scrupulously carried out their mandates as international civil servants. For twenty or thirty years they were rather unremarkable not to say boring institutions. The Bank ended its role in Europe and went on to loan to emerging Third World countries, again mostly for infrastructure like roads, ports or electricity. The Fund lent, as foreseen, to overcome balance of payments problems, and was paid back as soon as its government clients became solvent once more.

Then three events changed the tableau. The first was the takeover of the Bank Presidency in 1968 by Robert McNamara. McNamara was a former President of the Ford Motor Company and former US Defence Secretary during the

Vietnam War. He immediately set about overhauling his new enterprise. To make more funds available for loans, he floated World Bank bonds on international capital markets. Since the Bank, like the Fund, was statutorily first in line for all government repayments, these bonds were seen as excellent "widows and orphans" top-rated AAA bonds. Bond sales brought huge amounts of fresh cash flooding into Bank coffers.

McNamara's ambition, as staff quickly learned, was to "push the money out the door." Personnel would be henceforward rewarded not on the basis of the quality of the projects their loans financed, but on the quantity of funds they could unload on Third World governments. Those governments were only too happy to accept, and cheerfully bought a lot of white elephants or turnkey plants that soon broke down or became obsolete.

The second event was the petroleum crisis of 1973 when the OPEC countries successfully quadrupled the price of oil. Nonproducers were trapped. Instead of looking for alternative energy solutions, not much in evidence at the time, they imported oil at the new OPEC price and went into debt to do so. OPEC members in turn, like good capitalists everywhere, put their huge earnings in Western banks which had to pay them interest – that's what bank deposits are for. So the private banks needed to drum up new business themselves and started to peddle loans to the South, the only markets that weren't saturated, effectively recycling the OPEC deposits.

Governments borrowed from public and private sources, not just to buy oil or white elephants but also for arms purchases (never a productive investment, but pure consumption) and for costly imported goodies for the upper and middle classes.

Third World countries may have been imprudent, corrupt, badly governed and all the rest, but they had no part in or control over the third event, which occurred in 1981. Recall that one of the first principles of the Washington Consensus is to keep inflation under tight control. Although the first moves occurred under Jimmy Carter, Ronald Reagan's people took office with the intention of enforcing that rule. The Treasury Department suddenly set interest rates sky-high without a second thought for what the effects might be in the South.

The Southern borrowers had actually been paying negative interest, meaning that they were being paid to borrow, because inflation rates were higher than interest rates. Thus they paid back their loans in devalued currency. In 1981, because their contracts specified variable, not fixed interest rates, they were suddenly supposed to pay real rates of eight or ten percent.

It didn't take long thereafter for the first debt crisis to erupt, with Mexico as the unfortunate victim. Many others followed: they simply had nothing left in the cash-drawer. The IMF, soon joined by the Bank, designed programmes which were supposed to allow these countries to pull their economic socks up and retrench enough to begin paying back. These programmes included all the features of the WC and were called Structural Adjustment Programmes, or SAPs for short.

I often think how twentieth-century history might have been radically changed if the mostly Muslim OPEC countries had taken their religion seriously and refused to put their money in Western banks. They could have lent instead directly to Third World governments at no interest: Islam considers making money off a loan impious. But they didn't, and they indirectly put the Terrible Twins, along with the West, and especially the United States, in the saddle.

Thanks to the debt crisis, the Twins, in close alliance with the US Treasury, have been able to unite in imposing neo-liberal rules on less developed and heavily indebted countries, orienting their economies towards export production, refusing them all possibility of protecting their infant industries, privatising whatever meagre public services they had and dictating their budgetary choices in every respect.

Bank or Fund missions may go into incredible detail in their "recommendations." A large indebted country like Brazil will have more policy leeway, a small and weak African one precious little. One African participant in such negotiations reports that during a review of the health budget, the Minister announced his intention to recruit fourteen new public-health nurses. The World Bank representative shot back, "We told you you could only hire nine."

As underlined earlier, the Washington Consensus hasn't worked. It hurts the poor who got no benefit from the massive loans but must now make sacrifices to pay them back, it undermines vital government functions including education and health-care and it maintains a command structure much more efficient than colonialism.

Southern debt, a festering sore for the past twenty years, has relatively little to do with money and finance, and everything to do with the West's continuing exercise of economic and political control. Just think of the advantages: no army, no costly colonial administration, rock-bottom prices for raw materials because everyone is trying to export the same limited range of products – you even get paid a little. It's a dream system and Western powers won't abandon it unless their own outraged citizens – or a far greater unity among debtor countries themselves – oblige them to do so.

2 The World Trade Organisation

The WTO is the latest addition to the group of rule-making international agencies. Its official birth certificate reads January

1st, 1995, but it was a long time in gestation. At Bretton Woods, Keynes had hoped to make a trinity, adding an International Trade Organisation to the Bank and the Fund. Although it was negotiated in Havana after Keynes's death, the ITO never got off the ground. Too progressive for the Americans who refused to ratify the Havana Charter, it included provisions for using trade to reach full employment and even for agreements to ensure fairer and more stable prices for Third World primary products. The ITO charter was duly scrapped except for one chapter concerning industrial goods. In 1947, this became the General Agreement on Tariffs and Trade (GATT).

In a series of negotiating rounds, GATT member countries gradually reduced tariffs on goods from an average of forty to fifty percent to four to five percent, even though if it took them forty years. In 1986, they began another round in Punta del Este, Uruguay, but this time was different. After eight years, the "Uruguay Round" ended in the "Marrakech Agreement" (1994), a document approximately the size of the London phone book, and the charter for the World Trade Organisation.

The WTO is not the same kind of organisation as the Bank and the Fund, but rather an umbrella secretariat overseeing the implementation of the two dozen or so different agreements signed at Marrakech. These agreements cover not just industrial goods but agriculture, services, intellectual property (including patents on life forms), technical standards and a Dispute Resolution Body whose decisions are binding.

The WTO is also different in the sense that the TNCs wanted it, lobbied for it and were deeply involved in devising its rules. As the former Director of the General Agreement on Trade in Services (GATS) said:

Without the enormous pressures exerted by the American financial sector, particularly companies like American Express and Citicorp, there would have been no GATS and therefore perhaps no Uruguay Round and no WTO. The US fought to get services on the agenda....[23]

Pharmaceutical, biotech, software and entertainment companies were especially vigilant on the Trade-Related Intellectual Property (TRIPs) agreement whose rules were tailored to suit them; for example they extended patent protection worldwide to twenty years. This rule helps to prevent upstart countries from getting their hands on new technology and keeps them in their place.

One can't honestly say that the WTO was negotiated in secret, but citizens and their elected representatives frankly hadn't a clue what was going on. During the long years of negotiations, I was preoccupied, like most of the people I knew at the time, with debt and structural adjustment in the South and the rise of neo-liberalism in the West. Towards the end of the Uruguay Round, I attended a demo with Greenpeace people to protest the TRIPs and patents on life, but I had no idea of the full horror of the total WTO package. Except for the TNCs and the technocrats themselves, few people had their eye on these apparently dull, technical trade talks. How wrong we were!

And how right, once again, were the Transnationals. They knew what they wanted and got it. Some might say this is normal, since at least one-third of world trade isn't trade at all in the usual sense but rather intra-company exchanges (IBM trades with IBM, Ford with Ford and so on). A further third of world trade takes place between affiliates of different TNCs. In the WTO, the laws of the market take precedence over any other international law (for example, human rights or environmental agreements) and unlike the GATT, the WTO is empowered in many cases to supersede national laws as well.

As of early 2004, the WTO has 148 members (including China but not yet Russia). Formally, the rule is one country one vote; practically speaking, a vote is never taken and decisions are made by "consensus." This usually means that the "Quad" – the US, Canada, Japan and the European Union – have agreed so the others had better fall into line. The European Commission represents all fifteen EU countries, although the Quad took a beating at the Cancún, Mexico ministerial meeting, in September 2003, at the hands of Southern countries united in the "group of 20."

Many poor countries don't even have a permanent ambassador to the WTO in Geneva and none of them have the personnel needed to follow simultaneous, complex negotiations and committee meetings. As one Third World official remarked, "The WTO is like a multiplex cinema. You have to choose the film you want to see because you can't see them all."

First and worst: the General Agreement on Trade in Services (GATS)

Although many agreements under the WTO give ample cause for concern, I nominate the GATS for first prize with the Agreement on Agriculture and TRIPs on intellectual property as close runners-up. Like the other WTO texts, GATS is not exactly light summer reading, but once you work through the verbiage you discover it's a ticking time-bomb and a monster threat to citizens in general and to public services in particular.

World services trade represents about a fifth of all trade or nearly 1.500 billion (1.5 trillion) dollars, most of it earned by

US and European services TNCs. But what, exactly, is a service? The *Economist* says it's anything you can't drop on your foot. The GATS has divided them into twelve major sectors (and, for the moment, 165 subsectors): Services to Business; Communications; Construction and Engineering; Distribution; Education; Environment; Financial; Health and Social services; Tourism; Transport; Entertainment, Culture and Sports and, in case they've forgotten something, Other. Energy, formerly a good, has now been stuffed into Other.

GATS isn't a finished treaty but a framework agreement providing for a series of negotiations "with a view to achieving a progressively higher level of liberalisation ... [and] as a means of providing effective market access" (Article XIX). No one knows or indeed can know where the process might stop. The series of negotiations could continue indefinitely. GATS, unlike GATT, also provides rules so that services companies can invest in other GATS member countries and move personnel there on a temporary basis.

GATS defines public services, or "services supplied in the exercise of governmental authority," so narrowly that only the Central Bank, the army, the police and the justice system escape. All other services, if "supplied on a commercial basis or in competition with one or more services suppliers," are covered by GATS rules – like the post office and railways, schools and hospitals. GATS defenders tell us not to worry because no country is obliged to schedule any sector, that is, put it on a list of sectors and subsectors that it is prepared to open to foreign commercial competition. This may be theoretically true, but countries are put under heavy pressure to open up, as the so-called "Doha Development Round" GATS negotiations show. What they don't schedule this time they'll be energetically encouraged to list in the next round. The best advice in this regard was given by Nancy Reagan: "Just Say No."

WTO rules oblige countries to treat all other WTO members in exactly the same way (the "most favoured nation" rule). For example, the European Union, which used to give preferential treatment to its ex-colonies (the "ACP" or African, Caribbean and Pacific countries) was overruled by the WTO Dispute Resolution Body in the famous banana case which it lost to the United States. Do I hear you objecting that the US is not a notably large banana producer? Quite right, but Chiquita Brands, ex-United Fruit, is, and the case was brought by the US, with Ecuador participating, on Chiquita's behalf. It is doubtless purely coincidental that the CEO of Chiquita is a major donor to both the Republicans and the Democrats.

Thus the WTO can intervene in a government's internal affairs through dispute resolution. In the banana case it overruled an important aspect of foreign and development policy. It can do the same concerning government measures judged as "unnecessary barriers to trade in services" or measures which are "more burdensome than necessary." In case of complaints, the WTO court, the Dispute Resolution Body, not the country concerned, decides what is an "unnecessary barrier" or "more burdensome than necessary." In a judicial first, the GATS also orders member countries to set up special tribunals to hear cases "at the request of an affected service supplier" and provide "appropriate remedies" for a company unhappy with "administrative decisions affecting trade in services."

Let's imagine that under the GATS a member country government has scheduled or opened a sector, but some years later, after elections, the new government considers it to have been a disastrous decision: can it withdraw the country's signature?

Theoretically it can, after three years. But to do so, it will have to offer compensation by opening another sector judged by the other members to be of equal value. This opens such a can of legal worms that opening any sector is tantamount to a lifetime sentence.

In 1998, the then WTO director, Renato Ruggiero, summed up the situation:

> The GATS provides guarantees over a much wider field of regulation and law than the GATT ... [and extends] the reach of the Agreement into areas never before recognised as trade policy. I suspect that neither governments nor industries have yet appreciated the full value of existing commitments.[24]

Ruggiero may have been right about governments, but he was wrong about industries which have an astonishing ability to "appreciate the full value of existing commitments" for their activities and profits. Every time an official like EU Trade Commissioner Pascal Lamy blandly tells people not to worry about public services, he can only say what he *hopes* may be the case. He cannot say more than that, because as of yet there is no WTO jurisprudence on the GATS. Neither the Commissioner nor anyone else knows how a future WTO Dispute Resolution Body might rule.

Lurking dangers

Many other dangers lurk in the fine print of the WTO texts and we can't deal with all of them here. For example, the rules forbid members to judge products on the basis of "Processes and Methods of Production." If a football was produced by children in deplorable environmental conditions, it is exactly "the same" as a football produced by unionised labour. Beef with hormones and beef without are also supposedly the same. The agriculture agreement will lead to the ruin of even more small farmers; the TRIPs will slow technology transfer to the South while enhancing the control of Northern TNCs through patents and investment.

The WTO is also trying to add further areas of competence to the plethora of activities it already covers. Among them are a new agreement on investment, one on government procurement, another on "trade facilitation" (mostly getting rid of customs procedures) and finally one on competition policy.

Most countries of the South feel the WTO has put quite enough on their plates already, and have fought hard against these new issues. But the TNCs and the EU in particular are still pressing them. In 2003, I attended a meeting for interested citizens organised by the French Trade Ministry. The representative of the French and the European Employers' Federations (MEDEF and UNICE) said to the Minister:

> We think you have too many priorities. Agriculture, for example, contributes comparatively little to our GDP. What we want out of the next ministerial meeting [in Cancún, Mexico in September 2003] is an advance on GATS and a new investment agreement.

That statement should be enough to give progressives a clue to their own marching orders.

A lot of the horse-trading goes on in secret, or what amounts to the same thing since the minutes of meetings are generally not available for months after the event. Smaller countries are often excluded from major "Green Room" decisions (named after the wallpaper in the DG's office) in a process reserved for the happy and powerful few. In Europe, the shadowy "133 Committee" (named after the Article in the Nice Treaty dealing with commerce), made up of national civil servants, makes the decisions on services and does not publish its minutes.

In the movement, we've been reasonably lucky with leaks, and, by working with progressive Euro-parliamentarians, we finally shamed the European Commission into making public its GATS "requests" (sectors it wants other countries to open) and its "offers" (sectors it is prepared to open itself) which it previously refused to do. That's something; and of course even the smallest victory is welcome. But concerning an organisation which is in essence undemocratic and bent on driving the neo-liberal agenda forward, it's not enough. The WTO has got to be thoroughly, totally, completely overhauled.

3 The OECD and the G-8

The Organisation for Economic Cooperation and Development

The OECD is a rich countries' club. If you weren't in it and you're asked to join – like Mexico, Korea or Hungary – it means you've arrived, or you're politically useful. Originally set up to administer the Marshall Plan in Europe, the OECD later converted itself into a statistics- and study-generating talk shop. It was also the setting for negotiating the Multilateral Agreement on Investment (MAI). This agreement was torpedoed by the citizens movement in 1998, but it would have given huge powers to TNCs and subjugated states to their demands.

The OECD also contributes to formulating policy. For example, it has been pushing for labour "flexibility" for years. It developed a non-binding Code of Conduct for

Transnational Corporations and publishes a useful list of notorious tax-haven-plus-money-laundering micro-states which has pressured some of them to clean up their act in a limited way. The OECD website is worth looking at for certain kinds of information although you should be aware that if member countries don't like the content, they can intervene and censor the generally high-quality studies produced by the staff.

The G-8

The Group of the most rich/powerful countries in the world was first the G-5, then the G-7, and, now that Russia has joined, the G-8. The others are Canada, France, Germany, Italy, Japan, the United Kingdom and the United States. Valéry Giscard d'Estaing started it in 1975 as a fairly simple affair billed as a "fireside chat" in the Château de Rambouillet to talk about collective concerns and Western housekeeping arrangements like currency problems or the upheaval caused by the OPEC oil price rise.

After France inaugurated it, other members took turns hosting the meeting. Gradually the agenda and the meeting itself took on monstrous proportions – not only did the Five (Seven, Eight) anoint themselves to deal with the affairs of the entire planet, but the whole event began to resemble a potlatch.

Potlatches are rituals of North-western American Indian peoples who demonstrate their wealth by showing disdain for material possessions. At regular intervals, each clan tries to outdo the others, particularly those who are judged previously to have won, in the ostentatious destruction of wealth. Anthropologists have described these rituals in detail. Here is Franz Boas, the first to do so, in 1897:

The rivalry between chiefs and clans finds its strongest expression in the destruction of property. A chief will burn blankets, a canoe or break a copper [shaped copper plates that serve the function of money] thus indicating his disregard for the amount of money destroyed and showing that his mind is stronger, his power greater than that of his rival. If the latter is not able to destroy an equal amount of property without much delay, his name is broken.[25]

To my knowledge, no anthropologist has chosen to study the strange rites of the G-8, although it would be a fertile terrain for research. Like the Kwakiutl, the Tlingit and the Haida, each G-8 host country tries to surpass the level of splendour, complex organisation and expense set the previous year.

All this serves as the launch-pad for a puny communiqué, prepared almost entirely in advance by each government's "sherpas" – senior civil servants and diplomats who spend all year getting ready for these one- or two-day meetings. The generalities pompously expressed and the recommendations earnestly proffered are an unsurprising rehash of neo-liberal doctrine and promises to cast a favourable eye upon the lot of the poor (debt, AIDS and the like), virtually never followed by action.

G-8 preparation has become a relatively difficult feat since the global justice movement seized upon the meetings as venues for protesting the pretensions of these powerful leaders whom no one elected to manage the affairs of the world at large. The year after the Italian police went on the rampage at the Genoa G-8 in 2001, the Canadians put their meeting in an inaccessible village in the Rocky Mountains. The French chose the easily defensible spa town of Evian, hemmed in by mountains on one side and a lake on the other, while the Americans have picked Sea Island, a luxury resort off the coast of Georgia.

Protestors have understood instinctively that this informal organisation is an anthropological phenomenon (or a throwback to animal behaviour): the G-8's message concerns display, dominance and submission. The movement's message is: the G-8 is illegitimate and serves no purpose. We want a G-World, and we intend to be part of it.

PRIVATE ACTORS

1 The impact of the transnationals

By any measure, global capitalism in its latest incarnation isn't generous to the poor nor does it treat people and the planet fairly, but merely saying so seriously understates the problem. In fact, neo-liberal globalisation and human welfare are, at bottom, enemies. Just as in the case of the environment, they are incompatible for both theoretical and practical reasons.

In national settings, what economists call "Fordism" can work. Henry Ford was without a doubt a rapacious captain of industry but at least he grasped the secret of the system's success. After decades of industrial capitalism, nineteenth-century style, whose goal was to increase profits by squeezing the workers until they bled, Ford decreed "I pay my workers so they can buy my cars." Ford's workers made good wages for the time, whatever humiliations they had to suffer to receive them. (Ford actually sent social workers on surprise visits into employee's homes to be assured of their "clean-living.")

But Fordist logic breaks down at the global level. Transnational corporations often pay their employees better than most of the locals, but they also employ the smallest possible number of people directly. They have consistently reduced their workforces even as their sales and profits have soared. The international authority on this subject is the UN *World Investment Report*, already cited. Every year it charts the changes in TNC practices and gives the most accurate available picture of the cross-border mergers and acquisitions driving the corporate globalisation process.

I compared the sales and the employment figures of the top 100 corporations for 1993 and 1997 and found that while their sales had increased by over nineteen percent, they employed marginally fewer people (minus 0.7 percent) over that period. Since the companies on the lists of the top 100 were not necessarily the same from year to year, I also looked at the ones that were on both lists, by sector of activity. This was even more revealing:

SECTOR OR INDUSTRY	NUMBER OF FIRMS ON BOTH LISTS	SALES % 1993–97	JOBS % 1993–97
Electronics and computers	20	+16.5	-4.3
Automobile/tyres	11	+25	-6.8
Oil	11	+18.8	-24.4
Food, beverage, tobacco	6	+8	+1
Chemicals	9	+16.5	-15.4
Pharmaceuticals	5	+5.2	-14.8

Every sector but one increased its sales, often spectacularly, while laying off people in droves, especially in the oil, chemical and pharmaceutical sectors. The only reason the food and drink sector had a tiny one percent increase in employment was that McDonald's and Pepsi were hiring staff for fast-food outlets.

Using figures from different *World Investment Reports*, one finds that the world's top 100 companies, whose identities have changed to some degree over time, in 1993 sold 3.335 billion dollars worth of goods and employed 11.869.000 people. Seven years later, in 2000, after hundreds of mergers and acquisitions (M and As), their sales were 4.797 billion dollars and they employed 14.257.000 people. Thus, on the face of it, they increased their sales by forty-four percent and the number of their employees by twenty percent.

In fact they may not have increased employment at all: it's impossible to know how many staff they kept on after absorbing or merging with other companies where those people already worked. Furthermore, since 2000, the world has registered huge corporate failures, financial crises and massive lay-offs not yet reflected in the official figures.[26]

I'm always surprised when others are surprised at such lay-offs. An astonishing number of otherwise intelligent people seem to believe that the purpose of a capitalist economy is to provide jobs. The purpose of a capitalist economy is to make profits and increase shareholder value, full stop. If they happen to satisfy human needs, including the need for work, that is merely a by-product.

As trees shed leaves, companies are shedding workers. Even when the firms are making healthy profits they may have recourse to mass lay-offs because, as far as the market is concerned, people are not "human beings" with names and families but "labour" or "human resources" counted on the company books as costs, not assets. Despite huge investments in technology, labour is still the highest single cost for corporations and is therefore logically the top target for cuts.

Here is an example concerning well-known everyday products: Nike left the United States in the 1980s and went to Korea. When Korean workers struck for higher wages, Nike moved to Indonesia where, at the time, the going wage barely covered physical survival. Indonesian workers struck for better pay and when wages rose to 2.50 dollars a day, Nike moved part of its production to Vietnam. Like many other TNCs, it subcontracts to outfits that may sub-subcontract so it's hard for outsiders to know where production actually takes place.

The *World Investment Report 2002* says that "the existence of excess capacity in the order of twenty-five percent in North America and thirty percent in Western Europe has not stopped automobile TNCs from continuing to expand production capacity both at home and abroad."[27] In other words, this industry can't sell anywhere near the number of cars it can and does produce, yet it continues to invest in facilities in order to produce even more unsaleable cars. Overcapacity is also rife in many other industries.

Are these people crazy? Shouldn't the market – whose wisdom our neo-liberal friends never tire of praising – correct such an idiotic and wasteful situation of overcapacity and oversupply? Theoretically, yes, it should. But car (and other) manufacturers are now racing each other to reduce labour costs, that is, to get rid of people. So they invest in more expensive, fancy equipment to catch up with the best, like Toyota, which by 1997 could build a luxury car with only eighteen hours worth of labour content. The latest figure I've read for any company is just over fifteen hours.* Competition for market share is fierce, and in private top company brass will admit that inside of a decade probably only five or six automotive transnationals will remain.

Compared to the best, the plant that requires, say, twenty hours to build a similar car becomes obsolete even if it was completed the day before yesterday. Huge excess capacity results because, under these circumstances, it becomes logical to shut down plants that are *nearly* as efficient cost-wise, and build a new one.

"Nearly" isn't good enough. That's why Renault's Carlos "Cost-Killer" Ghosn was dispatched from France to Japan when Renault bought Nissan. Cost-kill he did, largely by getting rid of superfluous workers that the Japanese social system had always refused to regard as superfluous. Local culture must not get in the way of globalisation or profits.

More unemployment and lower wages also mean that fewer people can afford cars. This is so even in the bastion of capitalism where the average American family used to need eighteen weeks of wages to buy the average American car, but by the late 1990s had to devote twenty-eight weeks worth of income to buy an equivalent car.[28] Perhaps we should rejoice from an ecological point of view if there are fewer cars on the road but this is small consolation for the thousands of workers who have lost their jobs.

High productivity, i.e., the highest possible output per person, per hour, is what a company looks for, and here the transnationals are champions. Take the worldwide sales of the top 100 corporations in 2000, divide them by the total number

---

* Truck-building time at the Navistar Springfield, Ohio plant was reduced from 102 hours to 58 in only 2 years – and staff from 4800 in the late 1990s to 1100 in 2004.

of their employees and you'll find that from the CEO to the janitor, each employee of the top 100 is now responsible on average for over 330.000 dollars worth of sales yearly, up from 280.000 in 1993. Even if these figures are not in constant dollars, substantial gains in productivity have occurred.

It is virtually impossible for a smaller, national firm to match this kind of efficiency, whatever the industry. So it's not surprising to read in the *World Investment Report 2002* that "the entry-level requirements of competitive production are rising."[29] This means that the smaller firm is unlikely ever to have enough investment capital or to overcome its technological lag. It will never even be allowed on the same field as the major league players, at least not in mature industries.

The UN's most recent estimates (for 2001) count about 65.000 TNCs with 850.000 affiliates around the globe. Together they are making sales of 18.500 billion (18.5 trillion) dollars, or roughly half of gross world product. The largest 100 corporations alone make over a quarter of those sales, more than 4.625 billion (4.6 trillion) dollars. This is power on a nearly unimaginable scale.

Except for small nation-states like Singapore and Hong Kong, TNCs provide a relatively small percentage of local jobs.* And while you can arrive at least at a rough approximation of the number of jobs the large corporations create, there are no reliable figures concerning the number of jobs they destroy, which by any estimate is considerable.

We do know that these companies are merging like mad and buying up smaller, weaker firms; we also know that mergers

---

* The UN's "Transnationality Index," based on Foreign Direct Investment, value added and employment by foreign affiliates of TNCs, gives Germany, France, the US and Japan ten percent or less; the most dependent on TNCs in Europe are Belgium, Luxemburg, Ireland and Sweden.

and acquisitions almost invariably lead to job-shedding. These M and As now constitute more than eighty percent of what is confusingly labelled "Foreign Direct Investment." It's not investment in the usual sense at all, or at least not new, job-creating investment. Big-time merger-mania reached a peak in 2000.

Counting only cross-border M and As (not national ones) larger than a billion dollars, 175 deals worth 866 billion were clinched in 2000 (dropping in 2001 to "only" 113 deals worth 378 billion). For the decade between 1992 and 2001, the number of cross-border M and As came to 679 and the total amount spent on them was 2.500 billion (2.5 trillion) dollars. Imagine that a tax of a mere one percent had been levied on these deals in order to finance human welfare....[30]

M and As may not create jobs, but they do change the profit prospects for the firms that merge because they increase concentration, which is the same as saying that they reduce competition. Sometimes that is the only reason one firm buys another. Wherever financial crisis threatens to cause massive business failures, one sees the vultures circling, ready to buy up cash-strapped but still viable companies. After the Asian crisis of 1997–1998, the *International Herald Tribune* reported that American and Japanese TNCs were "snapping up" companies throughout the region. Workers who escape the axe and manage to keep their jobs are grateful for work at any price.

In contrast to the workers, the transnationals did very well during the years of the Asian, Russian and Latin American financial crises. In those halcyon days, the stock markets knew only one direction: up. The same sorts of people made the same sorts of predictions common in 1929, when Yale economics professor Irving Fisher announced that "stocks have reached a permanently high plateau."

Early in the present century, greed again carried the market balloon to giddy heights before it burst. Compounding market woes were the revelations concerning dirty corporate behaviour of which the single word "Enron" has become the symbol. Many other companies were implicated in similar scandals, especially in the United States.

2 The power of finance

Why do financial crises occur in the first place? Financial heavy-hitters – pension funds, commercial banks, insurance companies and brokerages – in 1995 controlled on behalf of their clients about 28.000 billion (28 trillion) dollars in funds. For the sake of comparison, the entire annual GDP of the United States at the beginning of the twenty-first century was between 10 and 11 trillion dollars; that of Europe about 9.5. I would like to give more recent data for the amount of cash controlled by banks, brokerages, insurance companies and pension funds (the numbers above come from the Bank for International Settlements [BIS] the central bank of central banks) but I haven't seen any in a while. Despite the financial tremors from the end of the 1990s to the present, it seems safe to guess that this astronomical figure has grown.

The BIS, reporting on the numerous financial crises between 1997 and 1999, speaks of market operators' herd behaviour. The really important players on these markets are a few hundred at best, and it's a pitiless milieu where everyone has an eye on everyone else. When an especially prestigious bank or investment house decides to flee, say, Thailand, everyone rushes for the exit.

While a relatively small fraction of their total money is invested in so-called "emerging markets" in the South, it helps to know that a mere one percent of the funds these mega-operators manage are equal to a quarter of the entire capitalisation of all the companies listed on all the stock markets of Asia (not counting Japan), or to two-thirds of all the capital value of all the firms listed on all the stock markets of Latin America. In other words, when these guys move they make huge waves and it's amazing, under the circumstances, that there aren't even more financial crises.

Until about the mid-1990s, it seemed that transnational capital could do no wrong – at least if you happened to be a wealthy investor. A financial crisis which was a disaster for the country concerned was not a crisis for the big players who always picked up their marbles in time or were bailed out by the IMF. From 1995, the IMF, using taxpayers' money, gave emergency crisis-stemming loans totalling 312 billion to Mexico, Thailand, Indonesia, South Korea, Russia, Brazil, Turkey and Argentina. Most of this money saved the major investors, not the governments per se and even less the ordinary people who lost their savings and their jobs.

The former chief economist of the World Bank, Joseph Stiglitz, has written a valuable book on how the IMF, a "public" institution, repeatedly got Northern private investors out of trouble.[31]

The kind of money that produces serial financial crises is called Portfolio Equity Investment or PEI (in contrast to Foreign Direct Investment or FDI). PEI means basically paper. People who purchase these paper assets don't care if the company produces cars, coffins or cheese so long as its financial results are satisfactory, or better still, spectacular. How those results are achieved is not the investor's concern. These assets are highly volatile. Since the 1990s companies have been more concerned by finance (again, "shareholder value") than any other aspect of their business including production.

Another aspect of complex financial-market games is currency trading. The well-known "Tobin tax" was a proposal to tax these trades – dollars into yen into euros into pounds into Swiss francs and round and round again. In the 1970s, when James Tobin invented his tax, currency markets dealt with about 80 billion dollars worth of trades a day. If that sounds like a lot, it's nothing compared to the figures now, which stand at about 1500 billion daily. Currency traders make, or lose, money by estimating how markets are going to value currencies relatively.

Currency markets are useful tools. Say you intend to buy a machine abroad which will be delivered in six months. You want to know today how much it will cost, so you buy a "position" in the currency in which you will pay the bill. That sum will be delivered to you on the agreed date, you pay your supplier and that's that. You don't have to worry about the euro going up or down fifteen percent between now and delivery.

But this kind of transaction in the real economy now represents only a tiny fraction of total currency trades (two to four percent) while the rest is pure speculation. As Keynes said, the froth of finance has grown far more important than the river of genuine economic activity. People make money off money with no transit via production and distribution. This is why the global justice movement is proposing a two-tier tax on financial transactions with a dual purpose. Invented by Professor Bernd Spahn, such a tax would, first, dampen speculation, and second, it could constitute a new source of funds to "aid citizens" as Attac says – and help us reach another world.

In normal circumstances, only the first tier of the tax would be levied, at a very low rate – say one tenth of one percent. In times of crisis with currency values fluctuating wildly, it would be applied at a much higher rate so as to stop traders in their tracks. The New York Stock Exchange has a similar mechanism. If stock prices drop too far, the market automatically halts trading. Technically a Spahn tax is entirely feasible.*

3 Lobbying for globalisation

Even though they often receive spontaneous help from the IMF or the G-8 governments, the transnationals and major financial players are also well organised to make sure their voices are clearly heard in the corridors of political power. In this regard, they have traditionally been way ahead of citizens.

For example, a major European lobby called the European Round Table of Industrialists has functioned since 1982 with a small secretariat in Brussels. It's not the permanent, coordinating personnel that gives the ERT its clout but its membership which includes some four dozen Euro-TNC presidents, among them those of British Petroleum, Shell, Daimler, Renault, Fiat, and Siemens. The ERT chose Brussels in order to have a direct line to the European Commission.

It has indeed frequently influenced the Commission's decisions. The researchers of the Corporate Europe Observatory (CEO) explain in detail how the ERT was able to shape the Trans-European Road Network (TERN), the Maastricht Treaty, the single currency and various "White Papers" drawn up under the Commission Presidency of Jacques Delors.[32]

* I'm grateful to Dominique Plihon and Bruno Jetin of the Attac Scientific Council for their clear explanations of this improved financial transactions tax.

As ERT member Baron Daniel Janssen, head of the Belgian giant chemical firm Solvay, told a meeting of the Trilateral Commission in Tokyo:

> The Commission plays the lead role in many areas of economic importance and it is extremely open to the business community, so that when businessmen like me face an issue that needs political input, we have access to excellent Commissioners such as Monti for competition, Lamy for world trade and Liikanen for e-commerce and industry.[33]

US corporate lobbies tend to organise along sectoral lines (federations for pharmaceuticals or chemicals, wheat or soybeans, etc.) and all of them maintain a cadre of professional lobbyists in Washington. No one thinks twice about the revolving door allowing high government officials to become lobbyists once out of office, or vice versa. Charlene Barshevsky, Bill Clinton's US Trade Representative (USTR is a cabinet-rank position for foreign trade), was previously a lobbyist for the Canadian wood and paper industries. Mickey Kantor, who preceded Barshevsky as USTR, moved on to defend the interests of the US Wheat Associates. At least two lobbies hardly need outside agents as they are now at the very heart of the US State: oil and armaments.

It is not unusual for sectoral associations to join forces temporarily or permanently to defend common causes. Thus banking, insurance, health-care, etc., all have their individual lobbying arms, but come together in the US Coalition of Service Industries (USCSI), an important player in the negotiations of the General Agreement on Trade in Services (GATS), under the auspices of the WTO. The USCSI has been working since 1982 to obtain trade rules favourable to its members' interests. It particularly wants to open all service sectors, including public services, health and education, to competition. This coalition rightly sees sectors like health-care in Europe as hugely promising potential markets, and it lobbies the USTR to push for privatisation and the penetration of US transnationals.[34]

The anti-environment business lobbies are numerous, especially in the US, where ecologists have replaced Communists as industry's favourite punching bags. As one US businessman put it, "environmentalists are like watermelon: green on the outside, red on the inside."

First published in 1993, the *Greenpeace Guide to Anti-Environmental Organisations* listed fifty-four professional associations and foundations, some with eminently ecological names, all lobbying frantically against any change in favour of the environment. One front group called the Global Climate Coalition was founded in 1989 with forty-six corporate members, including all the major oil companies. This coalition worked tirelessly to prevent steps towards CO_2 reduction in the US. As one congressman said, the group's only goal was the "unimpeded production of oil, gas and coal."

In 2003, I checked their website again. It announced: "The Global Climate Coalition has been deactivated. The industry voice on climate change has served its purpose by contributing to a new national approach to global warming." They can indeed claim victory. The Bush administration will continue to support "unimpeded production" and to oppose the Kyoto Protocol.

Another coalition of coalitions is the huge array of agribusiness, chemical, pharmaceutical and farm lobbies united in the effort to make Europeans accept Genetically Manipulated Organisms (GMOs). This fight was so important it caused a major debate in the US cabinet, finally arbitrated by President Bush. The outcome was the US challenge to Europe in the Dispute Resolution Body of the WTO to force open these potential markets. The Americans claim they are losing at least 300 million dollars a year in lost exports sales of GMO foods. Given the rules of the WTO, they will probably win their case.[35]

Some transnational public-relations firms like Hill & Knowlton or Burson-Marstellar specialise in worldwide anti-green PR campaigns.[36] Burson-Marstellar is also under contract to tout genetically manipulated crops.

When the GATS was being negotiated, between 1986 and 1994, the Europeans had no equivalent to the US Coalition of Service Industries, so rather than leave European TNCs in this sorry situation, without a channel to express their needs, European Trade Commissioner Sir Leon Brittan, with the help of the president of Barclays Bank, created the European Services Forum. It now has over eighty members and privileged access to the Commission.[37]

Another illuminating source for corporate-lobby fans is the International Chamber of Commerce, whose boss Maria Livanos Cattaui was previously a pillar of Davos. The ICC proclaims that it is "the voice of world business championing the global economy as a force for economic growth, job creation and prosperity." It goes without saying that free trade has iconic status at the ICC.

The least one can say is that the ICC and the then Trade Commissioner Brittan saw eye to eye on free trade. So perfect was their *entente cordiale* that it's impossible to tell who copied whom. Documents announcing the European position at the WTO (emanating from the Commission) and statements of aims of the business community (emanating from the ICC) bear an uncanny resemblance. Not only do they deal with the same subjects in the same order, but they do so in identical language, going on for paragraphs at a time about the liberalisation of European agriculture, patents on life or trade in services.[38]

Yet another international TNC lobby working for greater trade liberalisation is the TransAtlantic Business Dialogue (TABD), made up of industrialists from both sides of the Atlantic. The TABD has contributed a new word to the language: "deliverables," otherwise known as the list of items business expects governments to deliver.

Like the International Chamber of Commerce, the TABD makes detailed recommendations to trade negotiators concerning agreements under discussion at the WTO. It hosts a large annual conference, alternating between cities in the US and Europe, to which important political figures are invited. EU Trade Commissioner Pascal Lamy was the chief political invitee at the TABD meeting in Berlin a month before the WTO ministerial meeting in Seattle, and was also the featured speaker at the 2002 Conference in Chicago.

As soon as it was founded in 1995, the TABD set up "expert groups" (now about sixteen) on subjects as varied as aerospace, biotechnologies, chemicals, climate change or taxation. The corporations concerned meet to determine common harmonised standards for all their products, from heavy farm machinery to sailboats. The TABD's slogan is "Approved Once [by the TABD, who else?], Accepted Everywhere." Governments are then expected to ratify the lists of deliverables.

TABD designed this made-to-measure method to avoid costly regulation and to permit the same products to be sold on both sides of the Atlantic without further questions or restrictions. This is no small affair since US–European trade amounts to some 4000 billion (4 trillion) dollars a year.

Nobody – at least nobody official – seems to mind the concerted and generally successful efforts of TNC lobbies to be heard by negotiators or to participate in their activities. This is not surprising since transnational business *is* the priority of these officials who do their utmost to "incorporate" the corporate wish-list in their negotiating stance.

Even the United Nations has jumped on the lobby band-wagon – rather a blow to those of us who used to say, "well, A, B and C are all rotten, but at least we've still got the United Nations." Well, friends, the UN is no longer neutral. UN Secretary General Kofi Annan, with the help of Helmut Maucher, then board chair of Nestlé and also president of the International Chamber of Commerce, began cooking up a common plan at the Geneva Business Dialogue in 1998. This first step led some irreverent souls to refer to the SG as NesKofi. In any case, he brought to the Dialogue top personnel from UN agencies while Maucher selected the business brass, all of whom met under the auspices and with the benediction of the UN secretariat.

The Dialogue was only the prelude. At the World Economic Forum in Davos, in January 1999, Annan launched a ringing call to the TNCs to join the Global Compact, supposed to unite corporations and the UN in the quest for development. To become a member of the Global Compact, all a company need do is sign on for nine principles in the areas of labour or social rights and the environment. The Global Compact is halfway between a lobby and a laundromat for corporate repu-tations. The UN admits it has no capacity to monitor the overall behaviour of the companies that join the Global Compact; they can nonetheless drape themselves in the UN flag. One setback for the Global Compact occurred when the supposedly cleaner-than-clean Swedish executive it had elevated to a top position was obliged to leave under a cloud when it transpired that he had bilked his former company out of several million dollars for his private pension. On the whole, it would seem the companies get more out of the deal than the UN.

The curious case of Nestlé is instructive. The International Baby Foods Action Network, IBFAN, has been fighting Nestlé for three decades because it discourages breast feeding of infants in favour of promoting Nestlé powdered milk. These practices have resulted in infant health disasters in the South (dirty water, over-dilution, unsterilised bottles, etc.). A famous libel suit brought by the company in the late 1970s revolved around the charge that "Nestlé is a baby killer."[39]

In 2000, IBFAN wrote to the Global Compact director to ask if it was true, as rumour had it, that Nestlé was about to join. He said no, a thousand times no. In 2002, it turns out that Nestlé is now a member, and IBFAN wants to know why. Helmut Maucher must be pleased.

The latest fashion in corporate circles is a concept called Corporate Social Responsibility, or CSR. Dozens of conferences are held on this theme (I have attended a couple myself) and the stack of CSR publications grows higher monthly. Although many corporations have every interest in playing along, especially those with invaluable brands to protect, and although some are doubtless making a genuine effort to be "good corporate citizens," I still claim that CSR actually stands for Corporate Self-Regulation.

The TABD is a fine illustration. It defines its own rules of which the chief one is for governments to keep out, except to deliver deliverables. The goal is not just to keep governments out of the picture, but also to counter the growing demand, in which the global justice movement is a crucial voice, for *international* corporate regulation. The TABD is lobbying preventively against any steps in that direction.

In a CSR conference, when company representatives have just spent two hours boring you with testimonies to their virtue, and you finally get a chance to say: "Isn't the first duty of the good corporate citizen to pay his fair share of taxes?" they are dismayed that anyone could bring up such an indelicate subject. At one of these functions in Austria, a high-powered tax specialist on the same platform explained to me, as if to a small, not very bright child, that his job was to avoid taxes for his clients and that most tax codes allowed for this if you knew what treasures were hidden in their several thousand pages.

American newspapers sometimes publish stories about major profitable corporations that have paid no taxes at all over several years; some have even received government payments. A tax inspector I know in France says that, confronted with convoluted corporate structures and criss-crossed investments, his administration hasn't enough personnel to follow through. The head of a major foreign transnational in France asked by the administration to explain himself genuinely did not know exactly how many affiliates his company had in France alone. The conclusion? "They pay something, but they pay what they decide," says my friend. Private fortunes with savvy lawyers and bankers also pay proportionally little which leaves the rest of us to pay more.

Many other lobbies deserve attention. Some are straightforward employers' organisations like the CBI in Britain, UNICE at the European level, Keidanren in Japan or the National Association of Manufacturers in the US. Some specialise – for example, the US Council for International Business (trade) or the World Business Council for Sustainable Development (the environment) – but all are devoted not just to getting what they want for their own members, but also to preventing interference in what they see as their fiefdoms. Trust us, we're responsible. We can manage your affairs by ourselves. Citizen and government interference not welcome.

THE WORLD ECONOMIC FORUM AT DAVOS

The World Economic Forum is known to everyone by the name of its meeting place, the Swiss ski resort and site of Thomas Mann's *Magic Mountain*, Davos. For the days in January when it meets, it's more like the Money Mountain. CEOs of major companies, finance wizards, top government people and international organisation luminaries rub shoulders with a smattering of trade unionists, NGO stars and the occasional cleric.

Davos is like a kind of society hostess's triumph – nothing is actually decided there, but it's the contacts, the business cards you collect, the mere fact of being there that counts. I'm going because you're going, and you're going because you hope to meet X who will be there because Y told him he should go, and Y should know because he went last year and met Z for the first time ... you get the picture. It costs a lot to attend Davos meetings, and to be a member of the World Economic Forum at all, so you can show off in that way as well. Davos is definitely part of the consensus-building process of the conventional wisdom, but it never foresees anything and, personally, though I've never attended, I think it is sliding into decline and irrelevance.

Not so the Bilderberg Group, which is *really* exclusive – no publications, no publicity, no leaks and the major corporate and government decision makers attend because they can speak to each other with absolute frankness. "At Davos, you pay to see and be seen. At Bilderberg you go to listen without being seen," as one participant puts it. Another remarks – in English, of course – that it's "very white, very WASP ... Latins are no good at this sort of thing."[40]

Partly because of the World Economic Forum, the global justice movement decided it needed to hold a World Social Forum at the same time. So at least from our point of view, Davos will have served one useful purpose.

The citizens movement casts these public and private actors in a different role which we shall now examine: that of adversary.

4

...WE TARGET THE RIGHT ADVERSARIES

If things clearly need changing yet don't change, presumably someone or something is preventing it. If unemployment, injustice, poverty and environmental destruction reign, presumably there are forces that have a stake in perpetuating them. People who have fought for change over the years know that it doesn't occur spontaneously but only as a result of sustained pressure on the people, the institutions, the ideas that stand in the way.

Before any remedial action can be taken, one must first identify one's targets. Sometimes a collective effort and a democratic debate may be needed to do so, but usually the adversary blocking change and/or profiting from the status quo is in plain sight.

The global justice movement has coalesced partly because it has collectively determined who and what it needs to fight. No one should join this movement who disagrees on the targets already chosen for mass mobilisations – the World Bank, the IMF, the World Trade Organisation, the G-8 – not the only possible targets perhaps, but some of the ones identified for now. Here my goal is not to demonstrate that such institutions are in fact adversaries, as I consider this work has already been done.

Why "adversary" rather than "opponent" or "enemy"? Because "opponent" is too sportsmanlike; it sounds like Wimbledon. The movement isn't playing tennis and has to be free to make up some of the rules and tactics of the game as it goes along, and some of them may not be gentlemanly or lady-like.* "Enemy," on the other hand, suggests that nothing less than total victory will do, whereas nearly all political victories, as well as defeats, are partial ones. On rare occasions you can get rid of an enemy once and for all but you shouldn't count on it. An adversary, on the contrary is likely to be around for a long time in one form or another and the war will partly be one of attrition. Whereas you can beat an opponent and forget about him, or annihilate an enemy and never again have to think about him, fighting an adversary requires knowledge, political judo and long-term engagement.

THREE TRAPS

Before suggesting a quick method for identifying adversaries, let me try to get two common misconceptions out of the way and point to one mortal danger. I frequently encounter both misconceptions after any talk I give. Some good soul will stand up and announce that the adversary is actually ... ourselves. If the world is to change, we must change first. "We" need to correct not just our consumption but our ways of thinking and being, our very natures. Otherwise, nothing can happen at a larger scale. Another person at the opposite end of the spectrum, and the hall, will often retort that the shortest and best answer to "Who (or what) is the adversary?" is capitalism. Even if individuals want to change, they

* Although they should remain non-violent: see Chapter 10.

can't and won't until a revolutionary transformation sweeps them along in its implacable flow and allows them to exist in a post-capitalist society. That's an unsubtle statement of the two arguments, but it will have to serve. Both seem to me unhelpful.

Personal transformation

When I was growing up in the US, a popular comic strip called *Pogo* described the doings of a possum who lived in a swamp with lots of other intensely human-like animals. They were terrific, concerned about pollution and the witch-hunts of Senator Joseph McCarthy, and sometimes they held demonstrations. One of the swamp denizens' banners read: "We have met the enemy and he is us." It's a nice twist on the famous message sent by US naval hero Admiral Perry during the War of 1812, "we have met the enemy and he is ours," but it's not especially useful for the task at hand.[41]

When Pogo and his friends coined the phrase, they were surveying a dump littered with people's cast-off junk and were making a point about pollution, not about human nature. Different sorts of animals, real ones this time, can also help us to understand ourselves and, happily, Darwinian realities no longer shock most people. We can accept that we share many traits with our furry friends of the mammalian family, as well as some belonging to distinctly earlier species, including reptiles. Ethology, primate and zoological research shows that animals of many species frequently cooperate among themselves because cooperation represents their best survival strategy.[42] But they can also be rivalrous, aggressive and rapacious where important things like food, sex or territory are at stake.

Cooperation is surely the best survival strategy for humans as well, but humans sometimes go one better than animals by being downright perniciously evil, and not just over matters of food or sex. The adjective "bestial" has always seemed to me unfair as no animal would do what humans have shown themselves capable of doing to each other. What is civilisation if not the attempt to curb these base aspects of our nature and to devise ways of living together decently, with at least a veneer of culture and a modicum of enjoyment?

Although too often in our troubled times religion encourages self-righteousness and fanaticism, at its best it's meant to help us become less violent, more respectful of creation and more compassionate towards our fellow creatures. Individuals may indeed undergo remarkable transformations: when these occur in a religious context, the experience is called conversion. Saintly lore is full of tales of spectacular conversions, the most famous perhaps being that of Saint Paul struck down by his vision of Christ on the road to Damascus. George Bush often describes how his conversion transformed his dissolute life. But when the most powerful man on earth tells diplomatic visitors, as he is said to have done, that "God told him" to invade Iraq, it makes one's hair stand on end. What if "God told him" to hit the nuclear button?

Even making the generous assumption that conversion has uniquely beneficent effects on the convert, his entourage and the world at large, statistically speaking, we're never going to reach a critical mass of the "transformed"; at least not soon enough to make a difference in a time of historical urgency.

Furthermore, a capitalist society based on competition is not conducive to positive personal change, nor can people change in total isolation from society – here the advocates of revolutionary transformation have a real point. The Chinese sage Lao Tzu said "above all, do not compete," by which I think he meant that competition necessarily leads to intimidation and oppression of others, to the victory of the strong over the weak and the consequent fragmentation of society. In our world, in our society, nearly everyone is forced to compete – just going to school, holding a job or running a small business is enough to be placed in a competitive situation. "Nice guys finish last" and other pithy proverbs of the free-market culture say it all.

So I'm afraid we're stuck with Kant and his "crooked timber of humanity, from which no straight thing was ever made." If we're going to build another world, it will be from this crooked timber and no other, so we'd better start learning the necessary carpentry.

The only solution is revolution

The group that says the real adversary is the entire economic system may be right, but it's still a bit daunting to be told to fight capitalism, full stop. How can you fight a concept or a hydra-headed beast? It may not even be useful to recommend it, because fighting capitalism (or the consequences of capitalism, which comes to nearly the same thing) is what every progressive movement does whether or not it casts its analysis in those terms. The more one must contend with the effects, the more the causes come to be recognised.

Achieving any improvement at all is difficult enough without telling people they must bring down, preferably tomorrow, the most powerful and pervasive economic system the world has ever known; one which hasn't stopped deepening and extending its reach for the past 500 years. It's enough to discourage all but the most tenacious. Demoralising people is not what the movement should be about.

The chances of an all-consuming one-off revolutionary transformation which could somehow destroy capitalism seem to me remarkably slim. A twenty-first century "revolution" might, perhaps, occur in several ways, but the storming of the Winter Palace isn't one of them.

Where's the geographic fulcrum? Not even Wall Street qualifies as the only centre of capitalist gravity. Smash the World Trade Center and the financial markets are up and running in a matter of days. What's the agency? I don't see anything one could call "the international working class" waiting in the wings – this notion strikes me more as wishful thinking than reality. Nor do I see any other international, united vanguard class except for the nomadic corporate and financial elites who are not exactly potential revolutionaries except in the wrong direction. The global justice movement might later develop into such an international agency, and this is devoutly to be wished, but it's not at that point yet.

Call me unimaginative: I can barely visualise what such a gigantic one-off event might look or feel like, but history suggests it could only come about after a series of wrenching crises in which millions would suffer and thousands die – and not the rich and powerful either. Frankly, I hope such traumatic events can be avoided.

But we should at least try to think seriously about the possibility, if only because so many dedicated people live in revolutionary hope. Can one foresee a collapse of the whole rotten capitalist structure under its own sheer dishonest weight? So far, we've had massive and multiple scandals of which Enron is emblematic but hardly alone. Transnational corporate fraud has been revealed as routine – some of it is even "legal." Enron, for example, had established over 700 affiliates in the Cayman Islands and other tax havens.

All the players in the system seem to go along – bankers rolling over loans to clients they shouldn't have touched to begin with; "analysts" taking bribes to praise publicly company shares they privately despise; auditors signing off on all manner of manipulation; financial journalists hyping and lying; and government regulators snoring peacefully while ordinary people lose their pensions and their savings. The outcome? A wrist gets slapped here or there but nothing fundamental changes.

Throw in for good measure the North's attitude towards the South, characterised by the persistence of unpayable debts, the lowest primary commodity prices ever (thanks to the export-led, glut-creating, WC policies of the IMF and the World Bank), the misery of half the world and a war widely perceived to have been at least partly about superpower control over oil. This war provoked worldwide opposition and the closest thing we've seen so far to an "international revolt of the masses" – yet still nothing visible or durable happens.

The United States frequently seems to be on the edge of international bankruptcy yet is always pulled back from the brink at the last cliffhanger moment. If the capitalist system is so resilient in times of crisis and recession, how much more so will it be in more prosperous times?

One begins to wonder how serious things would have to get to bring about genuinely epoch-making change. "Really bad" might mean what the French philosopher Paul Virilio has called the "global accident." He doesn't specify what it might be but points to the vulnerability of all man-made creations and institutions. The invention of the airplane is also the invention of the crash; the computer brings with it the certainty of catastrophic information loss; harnessing the atom implies Hiroshima and Chernobyl, and so on.

A capitalist global accident could be a simultaneous crash of all the financial markets, precipitated, perhaps, by the ballooning deficits, budgetary and commercial, of the United States which might one day go over the edge, cause a panicky flight from the dollar followed by out-of-control devaluation, a frantic and doomed attempt to pay off US debts, and worldwide inflation followed by a monumental banking collapse.

Don't ask me if this sequence of events is plausible – your guess is as good as mine. Any such scenario is not, however, to be cheerfully contemplated, revolutionary hope or not. A global accident of this kind would entail massive unemployment, wiped-out savings, pensions and insurance; societal breakdown, looting, crime, misery, scapegoating and repression, almost certainly followed by fascism, or at the very least, military takeovers.

People are now also justifiably leery of revolution and other so-called "grand narratives" given the totalitarian systems they have engendered in the past, even when the participants began with the best of intentions. I was never a supporter of the Soviet Union, the Maoists or any other purportedly "revolutionary" Third World regime so I'm at ease speaking about them now that the gulags, the killing fields and the secret police that came with them have been exposed to the harsh light of day.

Unless and until one can be quite sure such horrors can be avoided – and I don't see who or what might guarantee it – Socialism plus democracy (not the same thing as social democracy) is for me the answer even though it may strike some adventurous risk-loving spirits as boring.

A couple of other scenarios are entertained by some people who hope to avoid the sort of universal trauma just described.

I think they derive from faulty analysis, but I mention them in passing.

Nostalgia for May '68, mostly on the part of people who weren't there, has led some romantics to claim that such an upheaval could come to us again, this time on a global scale. May '68 was almost entirely non-violent, at least in Europe. It had some undeniably far-reaching cultural effects and brought some temporary gains for working people, but politically it failed and fizzled out under the neo-liberal onslaught of the Reagan–Thatcher years.

Just for comic relief, I'll throw in another possibility for fundamental change: the rich and powerful decide they have now acquired quite enough wealth and power, thank you, and will henceforth share them with those less fortunate than themselves. Some people don't think this scenario fantastical and behave as if they actually believed such things could come about. We'll look more closely at this extremely remote possibility in Chapter 9 on Illusions.

The circular firing squad

If neither mass personal transformation nor one-off revolutionary change can be counted on to create another world, perhaps we need to be a bit more modest. If capitalism does one day suffer defeat, I believe it will be as the cumulative result of hundreds of struggles, not of some great global apocalypse. So I humbly suggest that we just have to keep on working to change the balance of forces in the most imaginative and non-violent ways we can find, while keeping an eye out for what history has on offer. But for pity's sake, let's be pragmatic and try to understand what *our* reality is without trying to make it conform artificially to past models. Above all, we must not turn on each other as has so often happened simply because we disagree on some final, definitive state of history which is entirely out of our hands.

The mortal danger, the worst of all fates a movement can suffer, is when its participants pick *each other* as the adversary. The worst of all temptations is to devote more energy to fighting one's own rather than the bastards outside. Freud spoke of "the narcissism of small differences." Lori Wallach, in a more contemporary, less psychoanalytic metaphor calls it the "circular firing squad" and it is deadly indeed.

Anyone who has worked in movement politics has at some point been tempted to jettison commitments or shake free of even the best causes because the infighting has become unbearable. Personal rivalries, selfishness and factional power politics often play a role, as do the refusal or inability to compromise. Frustration, bitterness and mistrust ensue and huge amounts of energy are lost. Who can this serve, if not the adversary?

One way to avoid such divisions is to refrain from questioning each other's motives. Who cares why so-and-so does such-and-such, so long as these actions are useful to the objectives of the group? Giving the benefit of the doubt should be an internal movement rule: assume, until proven wrong, that everyone wants the success of the movement, that disagreements concern how best to reach its goals. Another remedy for factionalism is more, rather than less, democracy, but this doesn't always work either. Outside arbitration is rarely resorted to in my experience but could be valuable in internal conflict resolution.

In long years of activism only once have I become so fed up that I chucked the group altogether and concentrated on something else (after which, perhaps quite independently of my departure, the group ceased to function – not a disaster as it had largely served its purpose). Sometimes the crooked timber can be very warped indeed. But fights may also concern genuine matters of principle or strategy. I may be wrong but I think this is primarily a progressive illness. The Right seems to understand unity. Or maybe they are just more ruthless about eliminating troublemakers and factions.

In any case, long acrimonious discussions about such arcane matters as whether to overthrow or abolish rather than regulate or reform capitalism strike me as dated and a complete waste of time; first because we're not in control of events, second because every victory I have ever seen has been partial and even then subject to revision. Measured from an energy-efficiency standpoint, politics, especially adversarial politics, is a hugely expensive machine which demands an enormous input to produce even a tiny output of change and, worse still, demands a sustained input merely to preserve that output.

The classic debates about revolution versus reform and everything in between aren't that important so long as we can agree to respect each other's struggles and see them all as contributing to worldwide change and a more just distribution of wealth, resources and power, both within and between nations. Capitalism will be shaken as a result, from a thousand different blows to its foundations. But we cannot say when and we cannot discount any efforts, even indirect ones, to that end.

I like what Kevin Danaher of Global Exchange says with his inimitable boundless energy: "Inside, outside, we're all on the same side." He means that we've got people in suits and ties inside official buildings talking to parliamentarians, ministers and civil servants; we've got people in jeans and anoraks outside in the streets blocking the access to the World Bank conference or the WTO ministerial. We've got variety and we should glory in it.

The movement needs each of us, all of our talents and skills, because the fight we face is multifaceted and deadly serious. I don't believe that capitalism has or can have a human face. If this system is liveable at all, it's because the gains people have won through long years of struggle have to some degree tempered its brutality. The present capitalist programme, known as globalisation, includes clawing back as many of these hard-won advantages as possible. And we shouldn't doubt that the major actors in this system will react like ferocious animals should they feel cornered.

Therefore, fighting capitalism means not so much a rhetorical attitude as supporting working peoples' struggles to keep the gains of the past and as far as possible to extend them. This, in turn, may mean financial sacrifice and acting in solidarity with people on strike, at the cost of some personal inconvenience. The unions may not always be right, but they are right a good deal more often than the employers or the government. In many places, including the United States, unions are still strongly discouraged and union members are systematically harassed and threatened. The ILO keeps a list of trade unionists murdered or imprisoned because of their activities; in the name of working peoples' rights, hundreds give their lives and their liberty each year.

The point of what we are all doing, wherever we are doing it, whether or not we see our actions in exactly the same framework, is to create spaces in which humans and nature can thrive, to make demands on the present system and force it to respond, to find the contradictions in it and heighten them, to bend it until it either gives way or snaps. Such are our concrete, realistic, everyday struggles but they are also visionary ones once they are understood as part of a vast edifice, raised stone by stone, beam by beam, by thousands of unseen hands working together.

ANOTHER WORLD IS POSSIBLE: WHO OR WHAT IS PREVENTING IT?

Now assuming we are smart enough not to fight against our natures, against abstract notions, nor, above all, against each other, let's speak more specifically about the adversary.

For the sake of convenience, here is a matrix that may help to break down the problem into categories (which may overlap).

GEOGRAPHIC LEVEL	PUBLIC	PRIVATE
Local		
National		
European		
International		
Planetary (Environment)		

It could be an interesting exercise to ask all the members of a given group to fill in the boxes and then compare the results. An adversary in the Local/Private box could be a company employing clandestine sweatshop labour (as happened in Los Angeles) or one against which a strike is planned. In the Local/Public box one might find a municipal project to site a toxic waste dump in a poor neighbourhood or to reduce, privatise or eliminate public transport. The locals obviously know best what belongs in the local boxes.

Here now are some suggestions for filling in the other adversary boxes.

GEOGRAPHIC LEVEL	PUBLIC	PRIVATE
Local	(…)	(…)
National	The state? Specific government policies, laws, some political parties + campaign financing	Employers' unions, some industry federations, large farmer lobby, parts of media
Regional/ European	Parts of European Commission (Trade, Competition, Agriculture)	UNICE, ESF, ERT Eurofarm lobby, Eurofederations of industries
International	IMF, WTO sp. GATS, World Bank, US govt. + US military, G-8, OECD, tax havens	TABD, TNCs, Agribusiness, financial-market operators, "Davos"
Planetary (Environment)	WTO, IMF, World Bank	Petrol/automobile/ chemical/forestry/ mining/nuclear industry

Although I've filled in the national and international boxes with my own options, I don't claim they are complete or that there will always be agreement on the choices, even among progressive people, even within the same organisation.

THE NATIONAL LEVEL

Assuming that the local level boxes can't be completed by outsiders, we'll start with the national ones. I've put a question mark next to "The state" because anarchists, if I understand their position correctly, would probably disagree with me that we need the state (although a far more democratic one) in order to attain many of our other goals. So is the state as such really our enemy? It depends.

The post-war state was not, in my view, the natural enemy of Europeans, but it is more and more becoming so. Unfortunately, it's one of the few targets we can strike, at least for the moment. Take the example of creating a tax on financial transactions. Where would it come from? From a decree issued by the United Nations? That sounds like a bad joke. A spontaneous decision by the European Commission? Ditto. A sudden burst of generosity and fellow-feeling on the part of the United States and its currency traders? Fug-gedaboutit, as they say in New York.

The only hope I can see is that European governments, as a result of well-coordinated pressure applied by European citizens, decide to make Europe the first area where such a tax is applied. Acting on European states is feasible – tough to achieve, but feasible. Acting directly at the international level or begging banks and brokers to tax themselves is clearly impossible.

Another example: the European Commission ultimately takes orders from its member governments. Even in the case of particularly successful demonstrations (Seattle 1999 against the WTO, for example), even when we can orchestrate concerted, Europe-wide actions to make the Commission change slightly its trade policy, it's impossible to act directly or durably on this institution.* The Euro-parliament has very little power. It can pass resolutions which the Commission may take into account, but is not obliged to do so. If you want to change the mandate of the EU Trade Commissioner, or any other Commissioner, you have to make the member states insist on it. There is simply no other agency.

To affect durably the WTO or other international institutions, you must also reach the member governments. The Seattle victory made the adversary more wary and was entirely superseded by the WTO ministerial meeting in Doha two years later. Pressure on individual governments again led to whatever debt cancellation has occurred.

I am well aware that states represent and defend class interests and are, as Nietzsche said, "the coldest of cold monsters," but I am also making a plea for using whatever tools we may have at our disposal. Democratic freedoms are such tools, not to be neglected and despised but cherished and kept in good working order. Let's not forget that people gave their lives to establish these freedoms. The least we can do is respect their struggles and their memory by using all the rights so painfully acquired. Someone once said, "democracy is not something we have but something we do." People who, for example, refuse to vote on the grounds that "they're all the same" seem to me God's gift to the neo-liberals.

---

* We did force the Commission to become more transparent in the GATS negotiating process but it would be hard to get much further by targeting it directly.

It's easier to act upon some governments than upon others, it's as simple as that. However woefully inadequate "left" governments may be, they are still softer targets than the right, which owes us nothing.

Governments, when it suits them, will tell you they would love to help you but are powerless to act. Such a tactic is generally used to keep citizens off their backs. In fact, states still have more power than they sometimes care to admit. Unlike the anarchists, I think we should hang on to one of the only significant targets we can actually reach through democratic channels. One reason people take to the streets is precisely because no democratic spaces are provided at the international level. Citizens have, for now, no say over monetary policy, trade rules and so on.

If you tackle the question of the state with people from the South, however, nearly all of them will reply immediately and spontaneously that their own government is their greatest obstacle to change. Only afterwards do they speak about the class that government represents and the undemocratic laws and practices preventing dissent, a free press and meaningful citizen action. Africans are particularly ill-used in this regard.

Southern societies often function on the basis of clienteles and networks. What we in the West are prompt to call corruption – granting unwarranted favours, using public money for private ends – they may see as the duty of any powerful member towards the other members of the extended family. Southern leaders are indeed often corrupt in the classic sense of stealing for private individual accumulation, although they have no monopoly in that department, and they may cooperate with the worst elements of more powerful Northern countries in harming their compatriots. In their defence, they are confronted with virtually irresistible pressures; even models of courage and civic virtue would have to bend at least partly to the will of the North and the institutions like the IMF that it controls.

Once when I remarked in a conference that Southern elites were closer to their Northern counterparts than to their own poorer compatriots, an Italian businessman said I was wrong. He claimed these elites were too corrupt to be reliable partners for Northerners in anything. Maybe he's right. But surely the way to fight both the elites and corruption is by democratising the state and giving power to ordinary citizens. There are ways to accomplish that, to which we'll return.

THE INTERNATIONAL LEVEL: IS THE MARKET THE ADVERSARY?

Conspicuously absent from my International/Private box is the market, which some would surely want to see there. Like the state, I don't think the market *per se* is the adversary. Markets are not necessarily capitalist markets and they can be useful in exactly the way classical economists claim they are: when they provide for (regulated) competition, encourage innovation and creativity, allocate resources and permit price-setting. I don't want to haggle every time I buy a loaf of bread or a book and I prefer being able to compare, say, different computers before I buy one.

The issue as I see it is not to abolish markets – even if it were somehow possible to get rid of an institution which has existed in one form or another in virtually every society since the dawn of history. Trying to ban markets would be rather like banning rain. One can, however, enforce strict limitations on what is and is not governed by market rules and make sure that everyone can participate in exchange.

If people for whatever reason do not have money of their own, then they must receive vouchers for basic goods and/or have the right to a basic income. In the South, scarcity indicators should trigger the removal of some goods from the market, like cereals or oils in times of food shortages. Such vital goods must be kept out of the hands of private traders who in conditions of scarcity will invariably gouge the public. Some basic necessities may not lend themselves to market relations at all, and should be classed rather as public goods. Water is an obvious candidate, but because such goods are also scarce, mechanisms must be applied to prevent waste – perhaps, in the case of water, zero or minimal cost up to X litres per person per day, with sharply escalating prices thereafter.

Public services should be by nature outside the market and every society should be able to determine independently what constitutes a public service on its territory. Education and health-care should remain unreservedly in the public domain and be provided to all; depending on the society, additional private facilities (e.g., religious schools) may be desirable. Many societies, if they had any choice, would place public transport, communications and energy largely outside the market as well. The point is that democratic debate should determine what's in and what's out.

Mainstream economists maintain that thanks to the market economy, consumers will profit from lower prices resulting from competition. When supply is not controlled by monopolies or tight oligopolies, they're right, but people are not just consumers. As employees, families or students; as sick, unemployed, disabled or retired people, they often need to be protected against the market as well. It's this balance that is difficult but vital to achieve. We also need to consider who is producing the goods that come to the market, and how. Any future system will require the creation of wealth as well as its distribution but this does not imply that they must be capitalist types of production and distribution.

If the market is absent from my International box, the United States is specifically present and it's in there because the US is not just a problem for Americans but for the rest of us as well. This topic seems to me of such vital importance that I devote the next chapter to it, and ask readers to hold off crying anti-Americanism until they've read it.

I believe that the present United States government must be classed as an adversary, probably the most dangerous and the most difficult of all to tackle because it is a threat to people, to the planet and to peace. Like being told to fight capitalism, it's daunting to try to fight the US government. We must nonetheless try, and make it one of our principle goals.

5

... EUROPE WINS THE WAR
WITHIN THE WEST*

I expect this chapter to attract imprecations and brickbats, to alert the "gotcha" squads of the politically correct and to provoke (false) accusations of anti-Americanism by some and Occidentalo-centrism by others, specifically of the sub-genus Euro-centrism. Too bad. Let me say right away that it would be pretty hard for me to be anti-American: as a twelfth-generation American myself, I don't intend at this late hour to turn against my forebears, family and friends, my schools, camps and colleagues, the history I learned, the constitution I studied and the values I cherish. I am, on the other hand, shocked and angered by the denial of that history, the tarnishing of that constitution and the perversion of those values so evident in the administration of George W. Bush, which I see trying to carry out a creeping corporate *coup d'état*.

There is a big difference between being anti-American and being anti- the present American Establishment or anti-corporate government. I am well aware of the great qualities of the American people whom I admire and work with all the

* Now much revised, this chapter was initially my inaugural lecture for the Institute for the Study of European Transformations at London Metropolitan University, June 2003.

time. Indeed, I hope I may share some of those qualities. What's more, the Americans I know are the first to deplore the corporate militarised state they now face which is busily engaged in reducing their civil liberties and in feeding the population propaganda through a compliant media.

As to Occidentalo-centrism, I hope I have enough friends on other continents who have followed my work over the years and who can bear witness to my deep commitment to the proposition that all peoples, nations and cultures have a unique contribution to make to that other world we call for.

But here we are going to talk geo-politics and power relations and try to put hard-headedness and strategy in the place of sentiment and wishful thinking.

The United States will be the last to join any progressive initiative, if it joins at all. The international institutions like the World Bank, the IMF Fund and the WTO largely obey its will. For all these reasons, and others we shall soon encounter, the present US government stands at the head of my list of our adversaries.

It's all very well to have inspiring watchwords, no political movement can live without them, but the moment we abandon rhetoric and become cooler, more critical and analytical, we must ask *under what conditions* is another world possible? Is this just another phrase to keep up the morale of the troops or is it a serious proposition? I believe the answer is indissolubly joined to the nature and future of Europe.

EUROPEAN LEADERSHIP FOR ANOTHER WORLD?

To put the matter bluntly, I don't believe another world *is* possible without a Europe conscious of its indispensable role, determined to remain faithful to, and build upon, its roots, its culture and the more positive aspects of its history, especially its post-war history.

Furthermore, unless we manage to construct such a European consciousness and, from that, a European social model very different from the American one, and unless we can use such a model as the basis for that other possible world, not only will another world not be possible but Europe itself could well turn into a backwater – one with beautiful churches, chateaux and good wines, but a backwater all the same.

If Europe doesn't actively and consciously play the role of counterweight to the United States, politically, economically, socially and ecologically, then everything that matters will soon be decided and overseen by an iron-fisted hegemonic American leadership with velvet gloves optional. European capitalism will at the same time become vastly strengthened.

Here are my premises: I think it has now become clear that the American Establishment will set itself against any significant momentum towards an ecologically sustainable, socially responsible, humanly viable world. Such a world can only be built through cooperation, by nations agreeing to play by the same rules, including rules to curb the power of markets. America has no history, particularly in recent times, of submitting to any kind of international treaty or outside authority. Even if by some fluke the diplomats accepted them, the present Senate wouldn't ratify texts imposing external constraints.

Along with Somalia, the US is the only country which hasn't even ratified the Convention on the Rights of the Child. When it does join a supra-national organisation with teeth, like the World Trade Organisation, it uses the rules when they suit and flouts them when they don't. This is not the America I once knew – or thought I knew – but it is the one with which we are confronted today.

The United States wants no rivals, not even regional ones. The people who make American policy are far-sighted, tough-minded and far from naive. They recognise the threat Europe could represent to US hegemony, particularly since the relative success of the euro.* So far as Europeans are perceived to be defending, or even inching towards, a different world, the United States will attack them, sometimes subtly, sometimes more overtly.

In short, American policy makers will wage war. I believe they are already doing so in any number of ways, because they understand as Europeans themselves do not the threat of an alternative worldview backed by genuine political and economic power. The United States recognises the potential danger of an entity which now has 450 million people with a combined GNP of 9.6 trillion dollars, as against America's 280 million people and GNP of 10.5 trillion.

No doubt the construction and the emergence of a different, rival model to that of the US will require high courage, outstanding leadership and enduring stamina. Perhaps Europe will fall short, or not even try, but without it, I fear the dream of another possible world will be proven to be just that: a dream. This is why Europeans, especially those active in the global justice movement, have a particularly heavy responsibility. Europe alone can challenge the United States, at least for the coming years of the present century. Once again, this doesn't mean that other continents, other peoples, have nothing to say about the planet's future or any contribution to make to it – of course they do.

* But already in 1992, Paul Wolfowitz, then Under-Secretary of Defense, insisted in his secret report Defense Planning Guidance that "we must maintain the mechanisms for deterring potential competitors from even aspiring to a larger regional or global role." Western Europe was at the top of his list of possible rivals.

Everyone thinks immediately of the demographics and increasing economic clout of China and India. Clearly their geo-political time will come but frankly I'm just as glad that time is not yet here. Given the choice, I want neither the present repressive Chinese model nor the religious warfare of the caste-ridden Indian one. Like the Asian tigers, Japan is a bit light on the demographics and has been endlessly struggling with economic stagnation. In any case, for the nearly sixty years since World War II, Japan has been governed by the Liberal Democrats who would no more turn against the United States than they would parade naked down the Ginza. Other nations like Brazil are centres of hope, and will undoubtedly provide us with valuable social experiments. However, for many reasons including their debts and their dependency on foreign capital and export markets, they are not yet free to act in other areas as they might wish.

So for the moment, that leaves Europe as the only place I can see outside of the US with the economic and symbolic power as well as the historical and cultural experience to assume leadership at this point in history for a different path and an alternative model, to which other nations could then gravitate. If my hypothesis is correct, the crucial questions are these: Can Europe propose an alternative model for the world? Can such a model be constructed, and if so how?

SHARED VALUES?

On both sides of the Atlantic many people, including Tony Blair and Condoleezza Rice, like to proclaim that America and Europe share the same values. This may be the comforting view, but I'm not so sure. Once most Europeans start looking seriously at cavalier American attitudes towards social or environmental protection, they see little they would care to share.

One might also recall that the present European Community was founded in the 1950s on the principle that conflicts should be resolved peacefully, through the application of international law. This is less and less the attitude of the American leadership which is attacking the Europeans on everything from their hostility towards Genetically Manipulated Organisms to the reluctance of some of them to approve of invading sovereign nations.

Americans, including those in high places, are growing more ostentatiously religious, not to say fundamentalist. Boundaries between Church and State are less and less recognisable. Meetings at the Justice Department and the White House often begin with prayers. Various American state governments have deleted Darwin and evolutionary biology from the curriculum in favour of "creationism" (the Bible as the literal truth) whereas we in Europe are becoming rapidly de-Christianised. We had quite enough religious strife over several centuries to want to keep God out of public affairs.

They have still got the death penalty, execute mentally defective people, boast proportionally the largest prison population in the world, keep foreign prisoners under deplorable conditions at Camp X-Ray on Guantánamo Bay and have reactivated military tribunals for the first time in fifty years. God knows (but let's still keep God out of this) Europe's justice system isn't perfect, but at least it has escaped from the Middle Ages. Shared values seem to be dwindling.

WHICH WAY? LEADERSHIP OR SUBSERVIENCE

Can Europeans rise to the occasion? If most Europeans in a position to impose their views do not merely acquiesce to the

American model but actively promote it, as so many are doing today, then it will be a uphill battle. Since the great Chinese military strategist of circa 500 BC, Sun Tzu, we know that the greatest generals are those who do not need to fight. What is the goal of war if not to make the adversary accept our objectives as his objectives? If Europe were led by fifteen or twenty-five Tony Blairs all having assimilated as perfectly as he has done the military, political and economic objectives of the United States, the war for another possible world would already be irrevocably lost.

Whereas the first step for Europeans would be to recognise the challenge that is staring them in the face, I am sorry to say that for the most part, it has been neither identified nor accepted. Europe is heading in the opposite direction from the one I would like to see. The only good thing I could discern in the war against Iraq was that it clarified the nature of the present US administration and set the stage for a remarkable, though perhaps short-lived, display of independence on the part of at least some European countries' governments and especially of their populations.

One could make an open-ended list of everything that's going the wrong way, wrong at least if one accepts my plea for the need to build an alternative European model as the basis for an alternative world. Here's a short one:

1. Enlargement will strengthen the hand of US supporters inside the EU. The Eastern Europeans are, understandably enough, still psychologically damaged by their experience of Soviet occupation and they are, for the moment at least, eternally and uncritically grateful to the rival superpower for winning the Cold War.

2. The unambiguous alignment of Britain on American positions in any and all circumstances does not favour the emergence of a competing model. Unless Britain chooses Europe over the United States, General de Gaulle will have got it right: we let the Trojan Horse inside the walls and it now refuses to budge.

3. The neo-liberal goals of the present European Commission are clear. It is business- and privatisation-oriented and the European Trade Commissioner, nominal Socialist Pascal Lamy, has been even more relentless than his American counterpart in trying to wrench concessions from the poor South and push neo-liberalism worldwide.

4. The European Central Bank wants to strangle inflation, period, even, and especially, when inflation really isn't the problem. One can scarcely conceive of this Bank undertaking even the mildest Keynesian expansionary programme. Furthermore, it doesn't have the power of the US Federal Reserve, so even if it wanted to, it couldn't take strong measures to make the euro a genuine alternative to the dollar.

5. At the international level, the World Bank and the IMF are now very much creatures of the US Treasury and instruments of US foreign policy. This is unlikely to change unless European countries combine their voting strength into a single bloc that could challenge the Americans' dominant position. I can discern no official recognition whatsoever of this problem. Nor are there any signs of Europeans forming a united front against the grand design of the World Trade Organisation to incorporate all human activities and life itself into the market place. The United Nations has been

largely neutralised and would be scarcely breathing if it hadn't been for French, German, Russian and Chinese diplomacy during the Iraq crisis.

As I said, this is an open-ended, easily expandable list. Such factors and others like them indicate that the stars are not exactly smiling on the emergence of an independent European model. Despite everything, however, I don't just go about mouthing the slogan "Another world is possible:" I actually believe it, while recognising that it's a very long shot and a fragile hope.

For it to become more plausible, European citizens, and through them, European governments and institutions, must recognise that it is *in their interests and in the interests of the planet* to liberate themselves from the ideological and political grip of the United States administration and set out on this journey. Two and a quarter centuries after the US Declaration of Independence from Britain, Britain and with it the rest of Europe must declare its independence from the United States. European citizens will have to spearhead this transformation because their governments will almost certainly not do so spontaneously. The stakes are high.

THE EUROPEAN THREAT OF A GOOD EXAMPLE

Most of the global justice movement is proposing what amounts to a universal European model based on taxation, redistribution and democratic participation like the one developed in Western Europe from the 1930s onwards, particularly during the post-war period. Despite the many assaults against it, this model still exists at least partially today. Therein lies the threat to the US.

No one would be foolish enough to claim that the European model is or was perfect. But it's better than the American one by a long chalk and the proof is that the forces of neo-liberalism in Europe, in alliance with those in the US, are fighting to destroy it and are gaining ground despite some heroic efforts to stem the advance.

Meanwhile, the US juggernaut is lumbering forward. On its home terrain, although I can't prove it, my sense is that so long as the Cold War lasted, the US had to maintain some social programmes since it could not be seen to treat its own citizens worse than the USSR treated theirs. Since the fall of the Wall, however, food stamps and other welfare programmes have been drastically curtailed, while the number of both working and unemployed poor has simultaneously increased.

I also believe that the United States does not want its own meagre and inadequate social system compared to anything better, like the one that still exists in Europe. Sad to say, the European Commission is cooperating to dismantle one of the most brilliant collective human inventions since the beginning of modern history. Would it not be a *casus belli* with the United States if Europe were to announce that its own social model could be affordable for the entire world, that the necessary financial and organisational resources exist and that Europe would take the initiative to start this process?

THE EURO-MODEL: ONE WOMAN'S EXPERIENCE

If, as I believe, the US is already at war with Europe, then like any other war, it necessarily has myriad dimensions – cultural, social, political, economic, financial and military. Here none will get the attention they deserve. But allow me to look at a couple of them through the wrong end of the telescope, with an individual, small-scale view of the European model.

My view of the role Europe could and should play in the world is deeply coloured by my experience as someone born in the United States who has lived in France all her adult life. I realise that allowing personal details to creep in to a geo-political argument is poor academic form, but I'm not an academic and I think certain experiences show that the personal is political, as we used to say in the 1960s.

One year in my family life, my three children and I were all preparing for one or another important exam, from my doc-toral thesis defence down to the baccalauréate for my youngest daughter. Only my husband remained beyond the grasp of the Ministry of *l'Éducation nationale* and the Sorbonne. We all got our diplomas too, but my point is that in the United States, such collective family attainments would have been unthink-able even for a relatively privileged middle-class family like ours. Tuition costs would have been staggering. I certainly wouldn't have undertaken my doctorate with three kids to educate as a priority.

Had the system been the same as in the United States, I doubt I would have undertaken my previous French university degree years earlier either (a *licence* in philosophy) because of the expense involved. So I can easily argue that without the French state educational system, I wouldn't have written this book and you wouldn't be reading it.

One more story and then I promise to return to geo-politics. This one is sadder, but also illustrates my point. In May 2002, I lost my husband after a long illness, repeated hos-pitalisations, a huge operation, intensive care, a convalescence which finally didn't succeed; that's the short version of a saga that lasted over a year and a half. Once more, the French state was there for us. We probably could have scraped together the required outlays had that been the only way to carry on, but we didn't have to. Because my husband's condition was officially recognised as a serious illness, he was taken in charge 100 percent by the health-care system and, most important of all, the doctors made all the decisions. No time was lost. He got what he needed when he needed it. I saw poor, sometimes immigrant families visiting patients in the same intensive care unit who were treated with exactly the same concern. No wonder the World Health Organisation has called the French system the best in the world.

Please do not write to tell me that both the health and education systems are deteriorating in France. I'm sadly aware of these facts and support the struggles of school and hospital personnel, but I am talking here about ideal types and about realisations which are demonstrably do-able and not just in France.

THE EUROPEAN VERSUS THE AMERICAN MODEL

These two personal stories illustrate for me the essence of the European model of social solidarity. Of course, my husband had been paying into the system for decades before his turn came to call upon it. Everyone contributes in proportion to their salary, and employers pay in most of all, so that health-care remains largely free for everyone, especially in serious cases.

Taxes are higher than in many other countries, yes, but here too you get what you pay for, in this case education, unemployment compensation and social services, especially for the poorest. In the case of education (and yes, I also know about the gross differences in quality among educational establishments), what you receive depends at least to some extent on merit, on how hard you work; in health-care, it depends on your illness.

Europeans fought long and hard for the rights that make life worth living, precisely those the Washington Consensus is so anxious to eliminate. Public services, from the post office to the metro and the trains, from the electricity grid to the water supply, are also based on principles that took a long time to establish. Variations exist on all these themes and citizens of some European countries are clearly better off than others, but the model, however imperfect, does exist.

Access to services is theoretically equal; prices for services will not be determined by market factors; at least some sources of radio and TV information will remain outside the purely commercial sphere; and so on.

The unfortunate Brits live in a kind of halfway house between the Continent and the United States. They may still have the BBC, but their ghastly and perilous railways are grist to the mill of public service defenders in Europe, gleefully if guiltily grateful for the shambles across the Channel which provides them with a vivid argument in favour of public transport. As far as public services are concerned, the British are worse off than virtually all their Continental neighbours and definitely worse off than they were before Mrs. Thatcher began her onslaught against public services and the unions.

Compared to the United States, however, Britain is a veritable showcase for the public sector. Most people in Europe have heard that over 40 million American families have no health insurance because it is neither compulsory nor "portable." Your insurance is not tied to a national scheme but to your employer, many of which have no health plans. You can take out costly individual insurance, but ask your American friends how happy they are with it. You will hear daunting tales of medical procedures – even ambulances – denied because the insurance company, not the doctor, has decided you don't need them. Getting proper care is an obstacle course.

As for education, tuition costs have become astronomical. An American woman I met recently is worried about the quality of the public schools in her neighbourhood although she lives just a few miles from the Pentagon. Private school tuition for her daughters would total 50.000 dollars; her two girls are five and eight. After that costs get worse. A good college like the one I went to in the US in the 1950s now costs about 40.000 dollars a year.

Continental European employers may complain about social charges and threaten to pack their bags and head for the low taxes of Ireland or the cheap labour of China. Some of them do pull up stakes and such competition is pushing down social standards; about which more in a moment. But employers don't mind when they benefit from well-educated, healthy personnel with good public transport to bring them to the workplace and efficient communications systems for marketing their wares.

Another traditional component of the European social model is inter-generational solidarity – cradle to grave institutions, from crèches to retirement homes, to take care of children and old people. Again, these arrangements are far from perfect and there aren't enough of them, but at least it's not the British situation where one child in three or four is born into poverty. Nor, thank God, the American one where infant mortality rates among minority groups in places like northeast Washington, DC are comparable to those of many Third World countries.

Finally, although few OECD countries are particularly generous in regard to their international obligations, Europe has still consistently outperformed the United States in Official Development Assistance (ODA) to the poorer countries, and a few, like the Scandinavians and the Dutch, have regularly exceeded the UN target of 0.7 percent of GNP to be devoted to ODA. The US contributes 0.1 percent.

This model, at its best, rests on solidarity, inclusion and a sense of obligation to those who can't work and to the less fortunate both at home and abroad. All these gains are under serious threat, often underfunded and attacked, sometimes by the European Union, sometimes by the comfortable classes in power nationally, sometimes by both. The ideal, however imperfect, remains, and recent social struggles have shown that people will fight to defend it.

It's easy to argue that if Europeans have copied the US and moved closer to the neo-liberal model, particularly over the past decade, this has nothing to do with overt or covert warfare and is not the fault of the United States. Perhaps so. But such an argument would discount the investments and huge ideological success of the US right-wing which has spent hundreds of millions of dollars over the past thirty years to finance neo-liberal ideas, attack the Welfare State and promote worldwide pseudo-solutions like privatisation. The United States continues to wage the war of ideas in which neo-liberalism plays the role of the one true religion. In any event, Europe is gradually moving closer to the American distribution pattern.

I argue that the European social model is a prime target of an intra-West war, but one can also discern aspects of a doctrinal religious war between two basically different societies. A significant consensus exists on both sides of the Atlantic that one's own societal choice is the best. The US has a huge defence budget and virtually no social services but the consensus is that people don't need them and can get ahead on their own. The American dream is still lively: in a recent poll, asked if their own income figured in the top one percent of all American incomes, nineteen percent of the respondents said yes. Another twenty percent said no, not yet, but it would do soon.

ECONOMIC WARFARE

A significant cadre of American organisations is working to reduce government to its lowest common denominator and to impose social conservatism on the whole country. Remember Grover Norquist, head of Americans for Tax Reform who wants to "get government down to the size where you can drown it in the bathtub"? Norquist is also a formidable organiser. He coordinates the activities of some 100 neo-con lobbying groups, bringing them together with key Congress people in his celebrated Wednesday meetings where they get their marching orders for the week. Europeans, at least so far, and as far as I know, do not behave like this.

One of the most difficult aspects of US–European warfare to analyse is that of finance. I am not an economist but my impression is that American officials know exactly what they're doing by allowing the dollar to depreciate vis à vis the euro. European countries, especially Germany and France, need exports far more than does the US to keep their economies healthy. If your goods become a third more expensive on international markets than American ones, you are not likely to boost exports. The decision of a few minor central banks like Russia's to hold part of their currency reserves in euros cannot counterbalance this added burden on exports.

Most Americans will scarcely notice the difference in the exchange rate because their euro-based consumption is

123

minimal and if they are members of the travelling classes, they will just stop or delay coming to Europe, thereby weighing further on Continental economies. The US Treasury may not shout from the rooftops "we have abandoned the strong dollar policy," but Secretary John Snow has defined a "strong dollar" to his fellow finance ministers as one that is difficult to counterfeit ...

The very least one can say is that if someone is manipulating something, it isn't the European Central Bank or even the City. The signs point rather to a US policy of devaluation with Europe as chief victim and overall loser, selling fewer goods to the US and other dollar holders, receiving fewer tourists and therefore coming under increased pressure to cut costs, above all labour costs and public services – and away we go, down the chute towards a devalued social model.

With a euro that had by mid-2003 gained about thirty percent in value since 2000 and could become even more expensive, the choice will be stark. This is no time for a failure of nerve. All the European lobbies we've described in previous pages, all the neo-liberal corporate forces are going to use the "competitivity" argument to get their way. They want "flexible" labour markets and lower taxes; they will refuse to adequately fund services for the mass of the population while maintaining high quality private ones for themselves.

Either Europe acquiesces to American pressures – alas the most likely course given the politicians now in power – or Europeans must start using vile language, words not spoken in polite company, like "protectionism" or "subsidies." There will soon be at least 430 million people in Europe and there are already twenty-five EU member countries, a number which could expand still further to take in the Balkans, Russia and some of the former Socialist Republics as yet not included. If

Europe makes an all-out and costly effort to bring these new-comers up to speed (as it did earlier with the PIGS – Portugal, [southern] Italy or Ireland, Greece and Spain), and then gives priority to trade between Europeans and to keeping jobs in Europe, surely this is a large enough primary market?

Europe must also give preference to the countries closest to it, particularly those of the southern and eastern Mediterranean. However, present WTO rules do not allow anyone to accord any trade preferences of this kind. Trade rules and European preferences would also have to be restructured so as to admit goods from poorer countries (especially former European colonies), beginning with foodstuffs, textiles, clothing and leather goods. The neo-protectionists who insist on "site here to sell here" policies have a real point. Why should we buy goods produced by our "own" corporations made by non-unionised, repressed labour in China or other distant poor countries?

At this point, the neo-libs pounce: "Aha," they cry, "you're against development. We knew it all along!" No: we will buy goods from anyone who respects the ILO conventions, the Kyoto Protocol and the Multilateral Environment Agreements. But trade can and should serve as a policy instrument. European policy should give precedence to enlarged Europe itself, to the greater Mediterranean and to former colonial possessions.

It's not as if the United States is above using trade in the intra-West war. Free trade is the bedrock of neo-liberal dogma and here the US brooks no backtalk. Robert Zoellick, the US Trade Representative, has informed the rest of the world that no one gets a trade and investment agreement with the United States unless they support US foreign policy goals across the board. New Zealand, for example, is beyond the pale for having refused its waters and ports to US nuclear powered ships. The Americans have long memories.

This is the same Zoellick who, two months after September 11, with help from European Commissioner Pascal Lamy, bullied the WTO ministerial meeting in Doha into signing on for the misnamed "Doha Development Round." He used impassioned rhetoric along these lines: "They could destroy the World Trade Towers but they cannot destroy world trade; a new agreement is the best way to fight terrorism."

Maybe so, but the South, as later became obvious, got nothing from this deal. It accelerated the Services and Intellectual Property Agreements (GATS and TRIPs) and began forcing through new deals on investment, government procurement and competition. If the Americans want all activities to be ruled by the WTO it is primarily because their interests are thereby served, with European help.

Through trade rules, America now aspires to control virtually our entire lives, from the movies we see to the food we eat. They have skilfully used WTO agreements to force other countries to grant twenty-year patents, including patents on their own native plants and species. Through the GATS, trade rules now insinuate themselves into all areas of human existence, including education, health, culture, public services, water, etc.

The US government has backed the claims of pharmaceutical companies which refuse to allow distribution of generic drugs against AIDS and other illnesses to Africa despite decisions taken at the 2002 Doha WTO ministerial meeting. Although the firms finally accepted a compromise just before the WTO Cancún meeting in September 2003, it is so fraught with conditions that AIDS victims are unlikely to reap many benefits.

The US challenge to Europe on the subject of Genetically Manipulated Organisms, joined by Canada and Argentina, claims the EU ban on GMO imports violates the provisions of no less than four separate WTO agreements (Tariffs and Trade, Agriculture, Sanitary and Phyto-Sanitary Measures and Technical Barriers to Trade). The WTO's Dispute Resolution Body named a panel to hear the case in August 2003 and it is likely to agree that EU restrictions are "unnecessary barriers to trade" costing the US over 300 million dollars a year in lost exports of GMO seeds and foods. Given the rules of the WTO, the challengers will probably win their case. The irony is that, inside the EC, Commissioners Lamy and Fischler seem to be on their side.

This case isn't so much about selling millions of dollars worth of American crops as it is about giving the right to American companies to sell and plant GMO seed wherever they like. The GMOs will proliferate and traditional and organic agriculture will gradually become impossible. Biotech giants like Monsanto could then sell their products every year to captive farmers locked into a system they never chose. The companies are so desperate for a foothold that in the province of Aragon, Spain, they are giving away seeds to farmers in a bid to create dependency. The WTO lawsuit is a direct threat not just to the food supply of Europeans but also to their freedom to choose their own agricultural systems. I hope that this time, the US may provoke a serious reaction.

MILITARY ISSUES

The military aspects of the war within the West are complex and in flux, especially since the invasion of Iraq. In a gesture more symbolic than practical – because US reach is so broad that militarily it doesn't make much difference – America intends to move its troops out of Germany and put them further East. NATO may have suffered irreparable damage as well – it's too early to tell, although Lord Robertson has bailed out as its head.

William Pfaff, extrapolating from a speech delivered by Bush's national security adviser Condoleezza Rice, thinks the new American message to Europe is clear: "There should be a new system that goes beyond the limitations of NATO."[43] Not only does America consider the United Nations irrelevant, but spokesperson Rice was in fact announcing that NATO itself is done for because it "incorporates an internal multipolarity," which, translated from geopol-speak, means that "some NATO allies have policy visions rival to that of the United States and competing values." Any alliance of equals, much less one of potential rivals, is out. Unipolarity is in. Well, now at least we've heard it from the horse's mouth.

Even more dangerous to Europeans is the significant number of their influential compatriots who, prompted by their friends on the other side of the pond, have suddenly discovered that Europe may no longer be "protected" by the US. Europe therefore needs a huge defence budget that must somehow match the American effort. The only response I can think of to that is "why?" Even if Europe were to sacrifice its entire social model to defence spending, as the US has done, it would still be behind the United States in ten years time.

But so what? Where's the enemy? Europe needs to invest in high-quality intelligence and closer cooperation between the 15/25 states, in defence against terrorism and in rapid deployment of specialised units that can help out in natural disasters or supply peace-keeping forces in trouble spots, but it should have no vocation for major defence spending. It can buy a lot more security with development cooperation, especially with Muslim countries surrounding the Mediterranean.

So, no, I don't expect the Chinese or the North Africans to invade Europe any time soon. We should never forget that the US finally won the Cold War by luring the Soviet Union into the armaments trap, forcing it to match US defence spending. I devoutly hope that Europe will not be so stupid as to accept a similar ersatz challenge.

THE FOUNDING PRINCIPLES OF EUROPE: YOU CAN'T HAVE IT BOTH WAYS

Geo-politically, the intra-West war became clear to all during the invasion of Iraq. In the seventeenth century, Europe's experience of debilitating wars finally led to the treaty of Westphalia (1648), consecrating the principle of sovereignty and non-aggression against a state presenting no threat to one's own national security. Three hundred years later, following the further traumas of two world wars, the European Union was launched, and this new Europe was founded largely on the principle of peaceful conflict resolution.

Great Britain, Spain, Denmark and Portugal (not to mention the Eastern bloc), by siding with the United States on Iraq, denied and trampled over the basic principle of the EU, thus helping to score another point for the US hegemon.

Trying to have it both ways and to hang on to a shred of principle, the US–UK axis fabricated evidence that Iraq was a genuine threat to their own security, claiming a clear and present danger which could not wait for more UN inspections and resolutions. Even more preposterously, they pretended that Saddam Hussein could have his wicked way with the West within forty-five minutes. Plenty of people bought the propaganda.

One of the most terrifying realisations emerging from this war was that up to fifty-five percent of the US population actually believed that Saddam Hussein was directly responsible for the atrocities of September 11. The British press and population were less gullible, but Blair's popularity nonetheless soared in the immediate aftermath of the war and seventy percent of the British population had a favourable view of the United States – a far higher proportion than on the Continent. The fall-back defence of this war, or any other, on grounds of defending human rights rings especially hollow. Saddam Hussein was not the only brutal dictator on the world scene and the US had long been one of his major backers.

America's continuing aggressive stance against second-tier powers like Germany, Russia and especially France reveals an Empire which will do as it pleases and no longer cares what anyone thinks. The idea that international law and the United Nations should be invoked and involved in conflict resolution is foreign to the American leadership.

Against the odds, I hope that US actions will provoke reactions among Europeans and rouse the desire for independence; that Europe will also take its own initiatives, which countries beyond Europe could then join.

European unity will be crucial and to reinforce it, European governments must crack down on tax havens and the black economy as well as harmonise taxes so as to avoid tax competition toward the lowest common denominator, as in Ireland. They should take the initiative on taxing financial transactions, more than half of which concern the euro and the pound, and use the product of international taxation to constitute a new fund for solidarity with the Southern priority countries and for maintaining and improving social services in the North. They should prove through incentives and through dissuasive legislation that it's possible to have a dynamic economy that still preserves and enhances the environment. A social model that is inclusive and not based on fear (of losing one's job, of old age, of illness, etc.) is the best guarantee of a successful economy and a cohesive society.

Europe should stop hanging back and waiting, hoping perhaps to convince the United States to join in collective endeavours for the betterment of humanity. This will not happen. Europe's choice is either to accept subservience to the Empire or to move forward in constructing a model which attracts the support of others and gradually isolates the US. European governments so far seem loath to give up the comforts of the past and step out into the cold, uncertain area of international responsibility. Many of them are just plain scared of the consequences of braving the most powerful nation the world has ever seen.

Despite the obstacles, there is still room for manoeuvre and here the global justice movement has a vital role to play. A British journalist once asked me why the "anti-globalisation movement" had grown up when it did and become a new and quite powerful actor on the international scene. I spontaneously replied, "because the bastards have gone too far." Sorry for the unseemly language but perhaps sooner than we think the hegemon across the Atlantic may go over the top, overstep the bounds and finally galvanise even the most timid Europeans into action.

If they want their governments to take this path, it is up to European citizens to act, to save and to enhance their model and their cooperation with Southern partners. Europe must be transformed into a genuine power which can make a reality of our hope that "Another world is possible."

WHAT OTHER WORLD?
VISIONS OF THE POSSIBLE

*"Whenever you find yourself in the majority,
it's time to pause and reflect."*

MARK TWAIN

All good ideas begin with minorities. Sceptics label all proposals for change utopian until one day they are achieved. Whatever their historical period, all defenders of a fairer and more equitable world are first ridiculed, then attacked, then finally grudgingly accommodated. If they win, their victories may be subject to revision. If they lose, they generally fall into history's memory hole. We may not have to fight again against slavery or for women's suffrage, but you never know.

Still, the world does change and the proof is that we no longer live in caves or in serfdom. Economic systems and relations of production change as well; even capitalism will not be eternal. I am often asked if I am optimistic. I sometimes reply with the famous quote from the Italian thinker Gramsci: "Optimism of the will, pessimism of the mind."

In fact, the categories of optimism and pessimism are quite foreign to me; I've never based my life or actions on a calculus of favourable or unfavourable outcomes. This quote from Václav Havel masterfully expresses the sense I share. He wrote it after long years in prison as a political dissident:

> I am not an optimist because I am not sure that everything ends well. Nor am I a pessimist because I am not sure that everything ends badly. I just carry hope in my heart. Hope is the feeling that life and work have meaning. And you can have it regardless of the state of the world that surrounds you. Life without hope is empty, boring and useless. I cannot imagine that I could strive for something if I did not carry hope in me. It is as big a gift as life itself.

One needs hope because changing the world almost always comes about piecemeal and takes time, often an unconscionably long time. Consider the story of Thomas Clarkson. Less well known than the abolitionist MP William Wilberforce, Clarkson personifies the kind of individual determination without which change would not occur. In 1787, he and eleven other men met in a Quaker bookshop in London to found a society dedicated to preventing British shipowners and companies from participating in the lucrative slave trade. At that time you could buy a slave in Africa for 25 dollars and sell him for 150 in America. Many a British fortune was built on this suffering.

To accomplish this first step towards ending slavery worldwide, Clarkson and his friends involved clerics, MPs and concerned men and women from all social classes; within five years 400.000 people were boycotting slave-grown sugar. After twenty years of struggle, in 1807, both houses of parliament voted to ban the slave trade. The abolition of slavery itself throughout the British Empire took a further twenty-six years, but when the Abolition of Slavery Act was finally passed in 1833, Thomas Clarkson was alive to witness it.[44]

I doubt that I will see my own hopes for the world realised in the years I have left to live, but I do not find this in the least discouraging. It is simply a sign that the battle we have barely begun is of huge moment, the stuff of history. Having experienced the conformity of the 1950s, the hopes, achievements and failures of the '60s and '70s, the selfishness of the '80s and the smirking greed of the early '90s, I am thankful to have lived also in this time of awakening and renewal.

WHAT OTHER WORLD AND HOW?

When the global justice movement says that *another world is possible*, this is shorthand for the following argument which I merely summarise here since it pervades the whole of this book.

For perhaps the first time in history, the world really could afford to provide access to a decent life for every person on earth – enough food, clean water, adequate housing, basic education, health-care and public services, as set out in the Declaration of Human Rights of 1948. Where would the money be found? Where most of it already is – in the international sphere, in the profits of mega-corporations and on financial markets; in the cancellation of poor countries' debts; in closing down tax havens and making corporate taxes mandatory; in making so-called "free trade" fair trade.

Another world has to begin with a new, worldwide Keynesian-type programme of taxation and redistribution, exactly as it took off at the national level in the now-rich countries a century or so ago. Such a programme would need to be administered democratically so that citizens would share the responsibility for choosing priorities and overseeing programmes for each country. Such a worldwide Marshall Plan would also kick-start the sluggish world economy as the New Deal did in the United States in the 1930s, and it would create more political space for people to determine what kind of economy and society they want.

I recognise the objection that even if the money for such a huge undertaking were to be obtained, it would still come partly from the profits of transnationals and from financial markets. Such a solution thus presupposes that these forms of production and exchange will continue to exist. Fair enough. But let's accept that we need a transitional phase. So much devastation has taken place in poor countries and major social setbacks in rich ones that a large injection of cash for reparations is necessary. Too many people are living in infra-human conditions right now and we can't wait to change the whole capitalist apparatus before doing something about it.

For sure, money alone won't do the job, but without it hundreds of millions are doomed to the merest survival. Meanwhile, as citizen democracy gains more space, we can be more inventive concerning the creation and distribution of wealth.

The global justice movement has already registered some stunning victories, even if these are not always visible to everyone, particularly to the media. A good part of the media is anxious to downplay the significance of this new actor. The rise of the movement is an extremely recent phenomenon, dating from about 1997–1998, although the appearance of the Zapatistas in Chiapas, Mexico in 1994 and the strikes in France during the winter of 1995 were important precursors.

After we got rid of the Multilateral Agreement on Investment (MAI) in 1998, an editorial in the *Financial Times*, citing a line from *Butch Cassidy and the Sundance Kid*, asked "Who are these people anyway?" I think the line may actually have been "Who are these guys?" but no matter: Now they know. What's more, "these people" have already changed the terms of the debate. We used to hear that taxes on international currency transactions were impossible. Now we hear that they "need more study." That's not true either, we have all the studies we need and they all conclude that technically speaking the idea is applicable right now.

At least in Europe one can affirm that the movement has gone beyond the stage of being ridiculed, although some politicians and the right-wing press still attempt to misrepresent and discredit its views. Particularly after September 11, many of them even sought to link citizen activism with terrorism. On the whole, however, the citizens movement is taken seriously and in most countries, with the blatant exception of the United States, is objectively reported on.

Corporate control of the American media can seriously hamper the movement because in many cases honest reporters are prevented from publishing. One reporter with Fox News pleaded with the manager of her TV station to broadcast a fully referenced story that was sure to anger agribusiness interests. He refused, saying "We paid 3 billion dollars for these TV stations. We'll tell you what the news is. The news is what *we* say it is." The reporter was subsequently fired. Scandalously biased *New York Times* accounts of movement activities and demonstrations border on disinformation, and the number of stories killed by the US media in general, either to avoid angering corporate interests or with the excuse of "national security," is growing steadily.[45]

NEW MOVEMENT, OLD GOALS

The global justice movement's goals are not especially novel, even if they are often expressed in novel ways. One of our major demands was first articulated in 1789 in the French Declaration of the Rights of Man and the Citizen. Article XV of this document says "Society has a right to demand account-ability from all public servants for their administration." ("La société a le droit de demander compte à tout agent public de son administration.")

Why should this be any less true at the international level than at the national one? Why are the World Bank and the IMF never called to account? Why has the World Trade Organisation never carried out an evaluation of the impact of services trade, even though it is mandated by the text of the GATS itself? Why should these institutions impose with impunity their life-threatening policies? Why can they remain impervious to public opinion and invulnerable to law on the sole grounds that they are international and inter-governmental?

Other goals of the global justice movement were articulated in the Universal Declaration of Human Rights of 1948, partic-ularly in Article 25:

> Everyone has the right to a standard of living adequate for the health and well-being of himself and of his family, including food, clothing, housing and medical care and necessary social services, and the right to security in the event of unemployment, sickness, disability, widowhood, old age or other lack of livelihood … Motherhood and childhood are entitled to special care and assistance. All children, whether born in or out of wedlock, shall enjoy the same social protection.

This is the same text which Ronald Reagan's Ambassador to the United Nations, Jeane Kirkpatrick, called "a letter to Santa Claus," going on to say that "neither nature, experience nor probability informs these lists of 'entitlements' which are subject to no constraints except those of the mind and appetites of their authors."[46]* It is time to inform Ms. Kirkpatrick that the world is now indeed rich enough to provide the planet with all the items listed in Article 25 and this is no myth.

The means to do so, as already indicated, must come from international taxation, genuine debt relief, crackdowns on tax havens and consequent recovery of taxes unpaid by corporations and rich individuals. Although we need international rules, we also need profound reform or outright abolition of the Terrible Twins and the WTO in order to start again from scratch. All these are targets of campaigns underway in many countries spearheaded by Attac and dozens of other organisations.

THE MOST DIRE THREAT TO HUMANITY

Despite their importance, all these campaigns pale beside the paramount danger facing the world. I am grateful to George Monbiot for pointing in one of his excellent *Guardian* columns to a book called *When Life Nearly Died: The Greatest Mass Extinction of All Time* by Professor Michael Benton, a paleontologist.[47] The extinction Benton is talking about ended the Permian period. What does that remote era have to do with our own age? Plenty.

---

* This demonstrated hostility to human rights as defined in 1948 may be why Ambassador Kirkpatrick was named head of the Bush administration's Delegation to the United Nations Commission on Human Rights.

Scientists have recently discovered that in geological terms this extinction occurred with terrifying speed. They have now accurately dated the age of Permian marine and land sedimentary deposits from all over the world and all the data converge. The strata show that very rapidly oxygen virtually disappeared from the earth's atmosphere. Vegetation and animals were done for. The Permian period was an age (about 286 to 251 million years ago) during which life proliferated. Yet only a few species from an astonishingly rich assortment survived.

The culprits were gigantic volcanic explosions in Siberia which spewed out sulphur dioxide and carbon dioxide. Although the subsequent acid rain didn't help, it was the CO_2 that nearly did life in for good. Because of the consequent temperature rise, vast quantities of methane frozen in the polar regions were released. Methane is a potent greenhouse gas with about eleven times the impact of CO_2 per molecule. Runaway global warming ensued, literally smothering or starving to death life on earth. How great was the temperature increase? Scientists can also answer that question with great accuracy: six degrees centigrade.

The UN's Intergovernmental Panel on Climate Change suggested that six degrees is the probable upper limit of climate change by 2100 but many climatologists now believe they underestimated the possible rise in temperature and that six degrees may easily be exceeded by 2100.[48]

We had better face it: another world is indeed possible if we keep up our runaway consumption of fossil fuels. It will be a world where humans are no longer around to complain. The real sense of globalisation is the recognition that this globe is just a speck of dust in the universe and the universe won't even notice if we wreck it. Our honour as earthlings is at stake.

While we are on the crucial subject of the environment, let's examine some other perfectly feasible solutions to persistent problems that could be easily eliminated in another world.

ECO-RESPONSES

The most urgent as well as most difficult task is clearly to wean the world from its addiction to petroleum. Public agencies (the World Bank and other regional development banks) should be forbidden to lend for any projects that will contribute to global warming. They should pool their resources to improve the cost ratios of alternative energy sources from wind power to solar to hydrogen fuel cells. They could sponsor a public research facility for energy alternatives and efficiency.

If the World Bank and the regional banks had gone for solar and other renewables in India, China and elsewhere, they could have single-handedly brought down the cost of the technology to the point where it would be competitive with cheap Indian or Chinese coal, even in narrow economic terms, without counting the environmental and health benefits.

So far, the Bank has refused to use its financial clout and to transform its loans into environmental assets for the entire planet. Why insist on making the same mistakes we've always made? Why not make all lending institutions head straight for renewable energy and low-waste systems and emerge at last from the nineteenth century?

Practical ecologists have already done much valuable work toward righting the energy balance; this is not the place to report on it in detail. One thing is certain: the technology both for conserving and for producing energy efficiently exists. Politics, especially in the United States, and corporate interests prevent its being massively adopted.

The environment is one terrain where unusual coalitions can be formed in order to make our economic behaviour conform to inescapable ecological rules. Not only do mass organisations like Greenpeace or Friends of the Earth have millions of supporters, but there are also major allies in business itself. The largest insurance and re-insurance firms employ in-house climatologists because they know that the increasing frequency and violence of hurricanes, tornadoes, hailstorms, floods and fires are directly traceable to global warming. From the late 1980s onwards insurers have suffered catastrophic losses and they want governments to reduce CO_2 emissions. According to the WorldWatch Institute, their losses for the decade of the 1990s exceeded 600 billion dollars. Some insurers now refuse to cover storm-damage risks in the southern United States.

Clean production is another avenue towards environmental sanity. Some corporations can be persuaded to cooperate if they know they can make money on the project. The Greenpeace Greenfreeze, a fridge without CFCs, has become a bestseller in Germany. The German companies got the technology free and sold it on to China and others. The 3M corporation, maker of Scotch tape, Post-it notes and hundreds of other products, estimates that it has saved over 500 million dollars by adopting 3000 different environmentally friendly measures. They call it the 3P strategy: "Prevention of Pollution is Profitable."

More complex and less frequently encountered is the industrial ecosystem, of which a prototype can be found in Kalundborg, Denmark. Here factories and farmers cooperate by linking their "metabolisms." The wastes of one become the raw materials of the other and the whole production process is based on recycling. The power plant recycles its excess heat as steam which powers a petroleum refinery and a pharmaceuticals plant as well as greenhouses and a fish farm. The fish farm's waste is turned into fertiliser. Ashes from combustion are used in cement making, and so on. Kalundborg was organised by the business community with no help or subsidies from the government and it has been built up gradually. Imagine the economic and ecological benefits if industrial complexes were designed from day one with such circular flows in mind (hopefully scrapping the petroleum refinery).

One could perfectly well create industrial ecosystems in which the production of waste would be structurally reduced to a minimum. Durable goods like cars, TVs and kitchen appliances could remain the property and the responsibility of the manufacturer with the purchaser simply using them for as long as she chooses. At the end of their useful lives, these goods would be returned to the manufacturer for disassembly, recycling and transformation. The manufacturer would thus have every incentive to find low-cost and efficient solutions to waste disposal and would build in waste-reduction to begin with.

Some products can't be recycled because they are intrinsically dangerous and have no cycle in nature: toxic chemicals, heavy metals, nuclear wastes and the like. In another, ecological, world, such products would be stored under public control with the storage facilities rented out to companies which would have to pay all the costs of storage. A suitably high price for this service would concentrate their minds wonderfully towards finding safer substitutes.

This model is not just one in which the polluter pays, but one in which the polluter takes cradle-to-grave responsibility for toxic and dangerous substances. The social and ecological costs of dirty and hazardous production would be internalised, forcing industry to find cleaner ways of doing things.

If industry doesn't decide massively to undertake such reforms itself – and for reasons already explained this seems unlikely on a voluntary basis – society must take control. The regulatory road does not seem the most promising or the most efficient. Between 1970 and the late 1990s, expenditures in the United States to control and reduce pollution and toxic wastes amounted to roughly a trillion dollars. Yet at the end of that period, the American environment was more polluted than ever. Regulations can also be dismantled, as happened immediately after the Bush administration took over (pushing, as noted above, his Environmental Secretary to resign). There has to be a better and cheaper way to get results.

There is, and it's called green taxation, based on the concept developed by the Cambridge economist Arthur Cecil Pigou in the 1920s. Pigou is not much recognised today because, unluckily for him, he always stood under the towering shadow of Keynes. His idea was not to increase taxes but to change the tax basis so that reforms would be neutral for business. The Pigovian tax concept is based on a simple principle: tax more what you want less of, tax less what you want more of. We want less pollution, energy consumption, packaging, waste and toxics: tax them more. We want more employment, investment and disposable income: tax them less.

The other Pigovian principle is to use taxes to internalise all costs now borne by the environment and by society at large. The beauty of "green taxes" is that they can not only induce clean production, a healthier environment and a healthier population (which reduces costs for everyone) but also motivate the search for the most elegant and advanced solutions in future-oriented, high-tech and high-export-potential sectors. They redirect the economy from "sunset" to "sunrise" industries.

Green taxes also encourage employment because firms make profits not by laying off workers but by reducing energy consumption and waste. The first national economies to act boldly on these principles will enjoy a huge lead and reap substantial economic rewards, not to mention a healthier population and a higher quality of life. This is a win-win scenario.

MONEY ISN'T EVERYTHING BUT IT HELPS

Suppose that international taxation of financial transactions, corporate mergers and acquisitions and industrial pollution are accepted; that genuine debt relief is granted and a pool of fresh funds is thereby constituted. Is that the end of the story?

Of course not; it's not even half the story even though it's what the movement has to fight for in the present phase. The most important part remains to be invented and it concerns managing and using the money. The pool of new funds, being international in origin, should be internationally managed. Probably the best option (but I'm open to debate on all suggestions) would be a new, small UN body made up of personnel chosen from the UN specialised agencies plus a corps of roving auditors. The auditors are especially important and must be permanent fixtures. Their missions should never include nationals of the country concerned. I could also see actors in the global justice movement, elected, say, by the participants in the World Social Forum, as rotating representatives in such a body.

What would be its job? After forty-plus years of largely unsatisfactory development aid, we've had an opportunity to learn at least one thing: you can't just hand over funds to a government and hope for the best. I'm all for national sovereignty, but I'm against stupidity, corruption and waste. The people in the rich countries who generated the new money to begin with have some rights too, and it's not neo-colonialist to say so. They have the right, and the duty, to insist that whatever international tax funds are spent in the sovereign state of X benefit and reflect the interests of the citizens of X as articulated by the said citizens. Therefore the sovereign government of X had better accept genuine democratic decision-making concerning national spending priorities as defined by its own people. If the sovereign government of X refuses to play by these rules, fair enough. It's sovereign. But in that case, it doesn't get any money. People object: "Yes, but then it's the people who suffer." Maybe, for a short time. But in most cases the opprobrium that would go with being left out, plus the incentive of budget relief and the sight of one's neighbours benefiting from it, would cause the government to change its mind.

If a country is to benefit from fresh development funds, the government should establish a council whose decisions concerning the disposal of new monies are binding. Citizens elect their representatives to this council (if necessary in elections monitored by the new UN body to guarantee fairness). Representation should be both geographic and sectoral in order to reflect fully the various facets of the society – farmers, women, trade unions, entrepreneurs, teachers, students, public-health personnel, and so on.

In some countries, these associations come ready-made as pillars of the regime. The local dictator has his tame trade union, his wife deals with the tame national women's association, and so on. Here I do become "neo-colonial," with no apologies. Lots of Northern NGOs, development and humanitarian agencies have been working in these countries for years. They know who's who and they know which are the truly independent elements. In consultation with the donor governments, they should be able to impose upon the local dictator the presence of these elements in the council.

Permanent representatives of the corps of auditors and the UN managing agency should also sit on this council alongside representatives of the government and, perhaps, World Social Forum observers. The government proposes, the council disposes.

A more limited structure of this kind exists in the participatory budget of Porto Alegre (and about eighty-five other Brazilian cities) where a portion of the budget is set aside for discretionary spending by neighbourhoods and a complex, pyramidal system of democratic representation sets the priorities. Waste and corruption have vanished because the neighbourhoods make sure they are getting value for their money. Porto Alegre's experience could be adopted/adapted by municipalities in many other countries.

Some original social thinkers have proposed low-cost ideas for solving problems common to many societies. One comes from the Brazilian educator Cristovam Buarque, whose hugely successful work in Brasilia's school district brought him the first national education portfolio in Lula's government. The "Bolsa Escola," or school stipend, is an imaginative programme which combats hunger, illiteracy, child labour and petty crime in a single stroke.

To educate kids, you first have to get them in the door of the school, but if they have to work so that their family can eat, that's not going to happen. Recognising this, Buarque found a way to pay families for sending up to three children to school so long as they attend at least eighty-five percent of classes. The equivalent of five dollars a month may not sound like a princely sum, but for families unemployed or on a minimum wage of about seventy-five dollars monthly, it can make a big difference. The programme quickly doubled the number of poor children in schools in the Brasilia area and has had immediately visible effects, including taller, healthier, better-fed children and a big reduction in petty crime since the kids are no longer hanging out on the streets. Presumably with children no longer working, more jobs also become available for adults, although I've not seen data on this aspect of the Bolsa.

Generalizing the Bolsa Escola throughout Brazil would cost only 700 million dollars a year to cover the poorest families. It could be considerably more effective if the stipends were increased, especially in the largest cities where five dollars a month doesn't go that far. But Lula has also promised to honour Brazil's debt payments on a debt that has already been reimbursed several times over. Payments on the 260 billion dollar stock of debt come to a cool 43 billion a year, or about three-quarters of all Brazil's export earnings. It is of course far more important that the banks in New York and the World Bank squeeze every penny they can out of Brazil than it is to educate and feed Brazilian children.

Another scheme invented by a Latin American social innovator is avowedly capitalist, or at least "petty capitalist," but it could give a great boost to millions who have no assets, or rather *appear* to have no assets. Pioneered by the Peruvian economist Hernan de Soto, it involves giving formal title and legal recognition to the property that people already occupy, even if it's a tar-paper shack in a slum. Owning a corner of a community, however poor, however small, can encourage improvements – which create employment – and can also serve as collateral so that the person can borrow a little capital, for example to buy tools to become an independent artisan.

Hernan de Soto's organisation calculated, for example, that the poor in Egypt had accumulated an astonishing 241 billion dollars worth of assets. To put this sum in perspective, according to de Soto it is fifty-five times the amount of foreign investment in Egypt and seventy times the value of all foreign aid received since the time of Napoleon. But poor people's assets are mostly unusable and unproductive because they are not recognised by any larger system. De Soto's three word answer to the question "How can the poor benefit from globalisation?" is: *Through property law.*

We who live in countries with identity papers and certificates of all kinds can scarcely imagine life without them. A friend of mine who had no acquaintance with development theory, made what I found to be an extremely profound remark. An art historian, she had gone to India for the first time to study temple carvings or bronzes or whatever and returned appalled at the extent of poverty and the sheer volume of humanity which is the everyday reality in India. Telling me about her experience, she said, "You see, Susan, these people aren't registered anywhere." How true, and until they are "registered," they can't make the most ordinary transactions which we take for granted. A title to property, any property, is a good way to start this process.

Another, better-known "petty capitalist" scheme is Grameen-type banks, named after the pioneer bank making very small loans to poor women in Bangladesh. These institutions are not without problems – they may depend on contributions to keep going and their interest rates tend to be high – but this baby is one that shouldn't be thrown out with the bathwater. Fix the problems, but keep the means for poor people to become self-sufficient. What's needed is to extend the Grameen small-loan concept to allow for collective borrowing for cooperative enterprises, not just individual loans.

FARMERS ARE STILL HALF THE WORLD

For three decades I've been encouraging policies to favour small farmers and help them improve their traditional techniques in order to produce more food for their families. Many more agronomists and ecologists than was the case in the 1970s are now working on agricultural systems for people who can't afford costly inputs. Their results in a variety of environments and farming systems are increasingly spectacular. In widely scattered localities with very different conditions, agricultural innovators have produced remarkable improvements in yields, sometimes by reviving abandoned local techniques, or through crop rotations, improved water-management or soil preservation methods.

Guess why you have heard over and over that Monsanto's GMO crops will save the world from hunger, yet you (probably) haven't heard about people like Professor Jules Pretty of Essex University? Because Pretty's research has shown, for more than 200 farming community sites in fifty-two countries totalling the size of Italy, that you can increase yields by an average of more than seventy-three percent using simple, cost-free techniques. In Africa, you can trick the corn borer into eating something even more tasty by planting weeds between your rows of corn. Rice harvests in Madagascar have been improved from three to twelve tonnes per hectare through simple methods, without chemicals or fertilisers.

You don't need Monsanto and Co. – in fact Monsanto is the last thing you need. The instigators and practioners of these alternative farming systems aren't going to make any money for the TNCs. All they will do is improve immeasurably the livelihoods of poor peasants on every continent.[49] So, clearly, the less said about them, the better.

Asked to debate some executives of biotech companies in 2002, I accepted the invitation and made them a proposal: If your Genetically Manipulated Crops are so great and if you really think they can contribute to reducing hunger, let's have an honest scientific trial. I'm not asking for the moon, but I challenge you to devote a mere five percent of your research and development budget to low-cost, low-input crop improvement methods like those recorded by Jules Pretty. GMOs are already widely planted in the US and some other countries, so after, say, three to five years, one could scientifically judge which methods produced the best results and at what cost, taking into account not only the input costs to farmers but also to the environment and neighbouring farms, measured against total returns for the producers.

I had no illusions that the business types would welcome, much less implement, such a proposal – I just thought it was worth showing that they didn't care about farmers or hunger, but only about their own profits. Governments, however, could undertake this kind of research. In France, almost no official agronomic research is devoted to low-cost biological systems whereas high-input expensive ones take the lion's share. Doing this kind of work, systematically, with decent funding, on the ground and in cooperation with the people concerned, could transform rural livelihoods.

WORK, MANUFACTURING AND SERVICES

Many people far more qualified than I have reflected long and hard on how work might be organised in another world. One of them is Michael Albert whose book *Parecon* [for "participatory economics"]: *Life After Capitalism* is being translated into several dozen languages. I recommend it as a thoughtful examination of the subject, though despite all the translations it may be more relevant to the American context than to others.[50]

I also recommend the collective work of my friends at the International Forum on Globalisation which has the advantage of pointing to the many things which could be accomplished at the local level. They are correct that food, schooling, health, banking and a host of other needs could and should be satisfied within the small radius of those who express them.[51]

I still somehow fear that, despite the faith of many Greens, the needs of a complex economy can't all be fulfilled locally and that we'll not be able to escape this complex economy. This is perhaps the real difference between the utopians and the realists. I consider my calls for international taxation and redistribution realistic, whereas demands to return to a simpler, more rural or communal era strike me as utopian.

I don't believe we can return to some mythical golden age and am not in the least bucolic (though I love eating the vegetables from my garden). I think lots of people will want to live in large cities and that we will continue to manufacture some distinctly large, complex and non-local products, for example airplanes – hopefully hydrogen-powered environmentally friendly ones. The future also requires large, medium and small enterprises and they do not need to be privately held, capitalistic ones. The structure of each product, of each need, should determine the size of the firm that supplies it. To stick with airplanes, I could see a rivalry more like that of the football World Cup competition than the present one between Airbus and Boeing, because it's true one has to have incentives, including material ones, to keep people stimulated to do better and improve their product.

For all domains, let's look at incentives for individual and team excellence and collective honour rather than capitalist profit and shareholder value as a reward. People need and deserve to be recognised for their work and a monetary award is welcome, but rewards needn't be only financial. What better way to honour excellence than to establish Nobel-type prizes in any number of areas? An illness of our present society is that recognition is almost exclusively material because we have institutionalised a perverse and pathological system. We do not need to keep it. If you got a "Nobel" for excellence in whatever field, you could have the right to fly a flag above your house or out the window of your flat. This could become an incentive as effective as the seventeen-bedroom monstrosities American executives, intent on conspicuous consumption to display their attainments, feel they must live in.

In the social sphere, there is plenty of useful work to be done, but capitalism won't pay for it. We have also abandoned the system of universal conscription which helped to integrate social classes (at least the men) into a common idea of the Republic. With its demise has come greater individualism. Let's have a year of social service for all young people, including women and with no exemptions, which they could accomplish between the ages of eighteen and twenty-five and which complements as closely as possible their career choices for the future.

SOLIDARITY BEGINS AT HOME

Assuming we need to kick-start another world by taxing large existing structures, like TNCs, but we don't necessarily want to keep them once we are further down the road, then we need to consider how limits could be set on the size of corporations and financial institutions and how they could be obliged to serve the needs of the communities in which they're situated. As things stand, TNCs take first place for loans, even from Third World banks, because they have more clout and may also be more reliable in reimbursing than local business. They suck up the capital available and local firms have to pay more to take out loans. Of course it's even more effective if you just get rid of the local banks altogether as has been almost completely accomplished in countries like Mexico and Argentina, where virtually all the banks are now American whatever local names they may retain.

Corporations used to have charters which could be revoked. Now they benefit from weak laws (and strong lawyers) and have a kind of eternal life no matter what they do. We need to return to a chartering system which can sanction companies for misbehaviour or for not following guidelines.

I have insisted here on what we owe to the very poor South, but what about the countries of the North where the new tax revenues will, ideally, be raised? Don't they have needs too? They certainly have, and although their citizens do not generally live in circumstances as dire as those of the Third World, they are still subjected to burdens they should not have to shoulder. It would seem entirely reasonable to hold back a percentage of the funds collected on their territory to solve their own problems, perhaps twenty or twenty-five percent. The most serious problem to be tackled in the West is doubtless that of increasingly massive unemployment, casual work and the poverty, fear and despair that goes with it.

Banks could perfectly well all be cooperatives, capitalised at the outset with taxes transferred from the present commercial banks. But at the very least, all banks should be obliged to set aside a part of their capital for loans to the poor and for business or housing loans to residents of their local communities, as with the US Community Reinvestment Act.

I was amazed to learn from Kevin Danaher that six or seven percent of the US economy, the largest in the world, is already substantially outside the capitalist system. Co-ops, associations, worker- managed firms and various other structures are already functioning. We need to study them, understand how they work and how they link up, and extend their workable ideas to other areas, other countries. In a general way, let's have a knowledge-bank of what works.

Ceilings on inequality of remuneration seem to me vital. The official Japanese figure, the lowest in the developed world, is five-to-one between top- and bottom-scale pay and, whatever its faults, Japanese society is generally regarded as socially cohesive. The "efficient inequality ratio" ought also to be determined by democratic debate.

Some poor immigrant neighbourhoods in Northern countries are actually ghettoes with jobless rates of upwards of forty percent. People living there are often victims of prejudice and say that sometimes just giving their address ensures that they won't get the job. Why not rebuild these neighbourhoods according to the inhabitants specifications – they know better than anyone what's wrong with their sub-standard housing – employing local people as labour. The worksites would function simultaneously as training courses so that young people could master one or several trades after several months of paid employment.

Whatever funds were added to the national budget through the collection of taxes on financial transactions, pollution and energy, or the activities of transnational corporations, would not be simply handed over to the Northern governments either, any more so than in the South. Northern citizens could also elect councils to carry forward their priorities. I would also like to see a scheme by which one could allocate at least ten percent of local taxes to a specific use. Competent people have told me firmly that such self-allocation for national income taxes is a bad idea. The wrong budgets would get most of the money – not health, education or research, as I idealistically suppose. I bow to their superior wisdom but am still for finding ways to make public finance more democratic.

One way to help reduce structural unemployment would be a two-tier monetary system. A part of everyone's salary could be paid in time-bound money, not valid after a given period, renewable each time it was passed from account to account. This would discourage "sterile" money and encourage job-creating spending.

I've already explained my priorities for Europe: rapid integration of the newcomer countries and privileged partnerships with Mediterranean countries and with former African colonies. This would mean among other things a complete overhaul – indeed a dismantling – of the World Trade Organisation. World-scale free trade can only lead to disaster, encouraging the "race to the bottom" and alignment on the lowest producer costs, no matter what the social or environmental consequences. Yet national markets rarely provide enough scope. Each major area of the globe should be able to define its trading relationships and rules, but they should certainly not be those of NAFTA (North American Free Trade Association) or the ones the US wants to impose on North and South America through the FTAA (Free Trade Association of the Americas).

We often hear from our adversaries "you don't want rules, you want the law of the jungle." That's not true, we want rules, but not the ones that now exist which were defined by tiny minorities. In like manner, we recognise the need for international institutions, but again not the ones we have now. We do need laws, simply because without them we in the movement will have to go back to square one throughout eternity. Sisyphus had a rotten life.

We're also often asked if we want a world government. Personally I don't, or, rather, I think it's far too early. In my view we've not sufficiently practised or even won the new democratic freedoms we need, and a world government would quickly be taken over by the same people, which is to say the wrong ones, who now run everything else. Perhaps the World Social Forum in conjunction with the World Parliamentary Forum could be the embryo of a representative body at the international level, but we are not there yet. Five years since Seattle is historically a short time. Let's give the vineyards their time in the sun before we try to harvest the grapes and make the wine.

Everything said here is a work in progress – my modest contribution to the movement's ongoing appeal to the collective imagination and to our collective will to create another world.

PART TWO

ANOTHER WORLD IS WITHIN REACH IF...

6

... WE INCLUDE EVERYONE AND FORGE ALLIANCES

Immediately following is some down-to-earth practical advice for people who are already in the global justice movement or who want to join it. It may not be the most accomplished of literary devices to begin a new chapter with recommendations that sound as though they come from the "Miss Manners" etiquette column in the *Washington Post*, but I've sometimes seen such bad manners in the movement that I feel I must try to cover the subject somewhere.

If you feel concerned neither by the size nor by the effectiveness of the movement, I suggest you skip the next ten or so pages and pick up with the sections about the invention of the social forum, or relationships with political parties, or that you go straight to Chapter 7.

Sorry to be so basic, but the fact remains that however brilliant our ideas, however excellent our proposals, if this movement is to succeed in changing the world, then it must have 1) numbers 2) organisation and 3) alliances.

NUMBERS: ATTRACTING AND KEEPING ACTIVISTS

We need numbers for the simple reason that enough people have to want change to force action. So we need to practise a minimum of psychology and a politics of inclusion. Most people are at least a little unsure of themselves and afraid of being a bother, or they may be worried about lacking the knowledge or the skills to be useful. The occasional outgoing self-confident spirit will come to you, but for the rest you will need to reach out.

People also don't want to offend. I, for example, am shy about telling the chair of the innumerable meetings where I speak to make a special effort for newcomers. You might think this would be spontaneous but it's not. The group has just knocked itself out designing and putting up posters, contacting the local media, distributing flyers at the weekly market to attract their fellow citizens to my talk, and when hundreds of them actually do show up, the sponsoring group often acts as if nothing out of the ordinary had happened. It's a great thing to fill your hall, so why let all these potential supporters evaporate, as they will do if they're not made to feel immediately welcome.

The seven commandments

After many years as a practitioner, I've now got my established religion. It has only seven commandments so it may sound more like the number of deadly sins, or as though you're being short-changed, but believe me, if they were all observed – a rare occurrence – many souls as well as money and grief would be saved.

1. Compose a single-page, clearly written handout giving the basics of your analysis, goals, strategies and achievements so far. Place the handout on every chair in your meeting place, or else distribute it at the entrance. It will include, crucially, contact names and numbers or an e-mail address,

time/place of regular meetings, if you have them, and a membership form. This is the same handout, updated every so often with a history of what you've accomplished and what you're trying to do now that you can use as general publicity in a variety of settings. A company would call this a mission statement and it's not a bad idea to have one.

2. At the beginning of the evening, the chair welcomes everyone, and has a special word for those who have never attended a meeting of your group before. You might even ask them to raise their hands if they've never come before and say you hope they will want to come back. That way regulars can spot them and speak to them later. If latecomers are milling about in the back trying to find a seat, stop the proceedings altogether and ask those with vacant seats next to them to raise their hands until everyone is accommodated. At least in France, people tend to avoid the front row. I tell them (but would prefer that it be the chair) that we know some may have to leave before the end of the evening, but they should sit anywhere as no one will think the worse of them if they do leave.

3. Even if it is in plain view, explain that there is a table at the entry where participants can get further information about the movement and, if they'd like, fill in their membership forms. Make sure this table is staffed by pleasant people who know how to smile and be welcoming. At least one person should be behind this table at all times, before, during and after the meeting (for latecomers and early leavers). This table should be clearly labelled and easily accessible.

4. Have another table for literature. Make friends with a local bookshop manager who is prepared to work late and sell mutually chosen literature (including books by your speaker if he/she is an author). Or you can agree with the manager to order and buy the books at a discount and sell them yourselves, with the right to return unsold copies.

5. Even if it's on your leaflet, announce where, what and when your next activity is, or explain that "we meet every second Thursday at six p.m. in the town hall annex." Announce what the programme will be.

6. Whatever your parents may have told you, never hesitate to talk about money. I find out if the hall was rented or given free. If it cost the group something, the chair should say so and tell the audience where to put contributions. The audience should also be encouraged to contribute to the overall work of the group even if they don't want to join. You can explain your expenditures (for example, you had to pay my train fare, get posters printed, and so on).

7. Do all this before the speech actually starts. I now refuse to open my mouth until the chair has done his/her job in these respects. Otherwise, it's astonishing how it only happens during the general brouhaha at the end when people are gathering their coats and umbrellas and part of the audience has already left. The only exception to this rule is if you will have to stack the chairs or otherwise rearrange the hall. Then ask anyone who would like to help to stay an extra five minutes (and thank them).

ORGANISATION WILL BRING SALVATION

From recruits to world-changers

Now let's hope that these hints, at bottom just common or garden politeness, have brought you droves of members. Then what? Some smart organisations assign a "godmother" or "godfather" to every newcomer, someone with whom they can have an enjoyable social moment as well as learn "who's who" and quickly come to feel more comfortable with others in the group. "Meetings meetings meetings" isn't a recipe for conviviality. Save time for the whole group to have coffee or lunch or a drink together, go on a picnic, bring in an especially good film (Mike Moore's are sure-fire hits).* In other words, make doing politics at least occasionally fun.

Give everyone a task. I had a dear friend who, until he was captured and sent to a concentration camp, had been a leader of the French Resistance. He was in charge of infiltrating agents into the ministries and public administrations, the railways, the post office, etc. He said the most difficult part of the job was not recruiting people – many brave French men and women asked nothing better than to risk their lives against the enemy – but continually finding something for them to do. Because he knew that if they didn't have a task – even a not terribly vital one – they would drift away and be unavailable when a real opportunity arose.

It's the same with any political movement, although we no longer need risk our lives for our beliefs (at least not yet, or in the part of the world where I have the good fortune to live). Good groups and their leaders will have a sense for what each

* *Roger and Me*, *The Big One* and *Bowling for Columbine*.

person is able to do and ask them to do it. Accomplishing something together builds confidence and as confidence grows, individuals can take on different or more difficult jobs.

One of these jobs must be media relations because information can't be limited just to those who show up for the evening. Not all of the media will love you or print/broadcast news about you, but you should be fair and impartial whatever their political colour, give them a bio and an opportunity to interview your guest speaker or attend your action. You should prepare a proper press release, never longer than a page, which includes a "hook" – the salient fact or event that will be of enough interest to others that the journalist can lead with it.

The part of the citizens' movement I work with most closely, Attac-France, calls itself "a movement for popular education turned towards action." "Education populaire" has a long and honourable history in France dating from the nineteenth century, before universal, free and compulsory education was decreed. We still need it. The trick is balancing education and action. It's important to invite speakers who can explain particular issues clearly in order to engage one's fellow citizens and build a base for action, but some group members may complain that organising public talks doesn't qualify as "action." Ask them to suggest a certain number of well-targeted actions themselves for the rest of the group to discuss and choose among.

At Attac we've also instituted a commission system so that people who are interested in a particular campaign or area can meet and strategise with each other at regular intervals. These commissions are a good way to broaden the base of expertise. We hold day-long or weekend training sessions in order to increase the pool of competent speakers on particular issues and run a five-day "summer university" where 900 people turn up and take notes for six or seven hours a day. We never cease to be amazed at their stamina.

The scourge of jargon

Have you ever found yourself in a group where it seems that everyone but you knows what's going on? Have you felt like a rank outsider because the topics and the vocabulary were unfamiliar; or been afraid to open your mouth for fear of seeming a fool? I have. First when, with no experience, I began trying to act against the Vietnam War with seasoned political activists and also later when I started trying to understand the power relationships between North and South, the reasons for world hunger and poverty, the ravages of Third World debt, and the workings of major international institutions.

Some people use specialised language in order to communicate faster with each other (for example, one doctor explaining to another a patient's complex condition), but others may consciously or unconsciously use jargon to impress or to exclude. Some may simply be unable to imagine that others do not share their vocabulary, concepts and intellectual framework. The impact on the newcomer is, in any event, the same: disastrous. Whatever the motives (and the extenuating circumstances) of that incomprehensible, usually boring person across the table or up on the platform, it's no fun to feel inferior and left out.

Most people wouldn't feel excluded if they didn't fully understand the doctors' exchange but since we're supposed to be dealing with everyday reality here, it's easy to decide that perhaps one actually is inferior and dumber than the next person. The temptation is to leave quietly and renounce any future part in the discussions of Group X or the activities of Association Y. How could one possibly mingle with these extraordinary beings who not only know what they're talking about, but are talking about it fluently?

The first rule for the seasoned activist is: watch your language. Listen to yourself with one ear and assess your discourse critically. Are you using difficult language and specialised concepts you don't bother to explain? Referring to authors as if everyone knew who they were and had read them? Going too fast and assuming more rapport with the audience than you should? Going into too much detail for the circumstances? Listen – to yourself and your friends.

For the newcomer, the first rule is: relax. It's a bit like the situation I faced when I was worried about how to care for my first baby in a foreign country (Morocco) far from family and friends. The famous Doctor Benjamin Spock helped by saying in the opening paragraph of his *Baby and Child Care*, "you already know more than you think you do."

It's the same with globalisation or activism, and what you don't know now you can easily learn. You may not become an expert on any particular issue, although that too is entirely possible, but you can be someone who listens intelligently, speaks confidently and acts effectively for a common purpose. I hope that the first part of this book may have already helped you to do all three.

To pay or not to pay

Some Attac groups in other countries don't have paying memberships. In France we do because we think a financial contribution is important. Political action is never cost-free and we want to depend on our members rather than on fickle subsidies or grants. We recommend a yearly contribution according to income level, but people are naturally left free to choose between a bare minimum (students, unemployed) and the sky's the limit.

Attac-Germany does what I've unsuccessfully recommended to Attac-France* for years, and they say it makes all the difference: ask people to sign up for automatic bank transfers (monthly, quarterly or yearly) to the association. Like millions of others, I use this method to pay telephone and electricity bills and would much prefer using it to contribute to the organisations I support as well. I never remember when I'm due to pay my membership dues again, and since we entered the era of e-mail, writing the cheque and the address and posting it seem to me ever more onerous and easily put off. I'm pretty sure many others are like me, so if your country has an automatic payment system, use it.

Now let's assume you have been open and welcoming, eschewed jargon, helped every newcomer to feel at home, established a solid membership, good fellow-feeling and healthy finances in your group. Is that enough? "No," we are all supposed to sing out in unison, and this gives me a nice transition to the part about Alliances.

ALLIANCES

Practically everyone can agree that another world is necessary and urgent, that building it will take patience and intelligence and that it won't come about spontaneously. Not everyone agrees on how to do it.

I certainly don't have all the answers, and many of them will depend on the local/national culture anyway, but I am sure that

* Which will adopt this method in 2005: Hurrah.

"alliance" is a key word. As I've stressed at many points in these pages, politics is becoming more complicated and the nature of change-agents is also changing. At the end of *The Lugano Report*, when I wrote that small-business people could sometimes join alliances, various harder-line Marxists neglected the entire message of the book in order to zero in on, and denounce, that single phrase. Sorry, harder-line Marxist friends, but I think that's dumb. I didn't say, as I recall, that they could "always" or "automatically" be useful to alliances, but that in some cases they could.

Imagine that your local, regional or national government is toying with the idea of letting in Wal-Mart. Under WTO rules this is an entirely plausible scenario because "distribution" of all kinds is regulated by GATS. If you don't know what Wal-Mart is, ask any American. It's a chain of gigantic, warehouse-style no-frills stores that stock everything. There are already 3000 of them in the US and 1200 abroad. They pay their 780.000 employees as little as possible (many of them have to rely on food-stamps), treat them like dirt and do not allow unions. Their buyers scour the world for the cheapest prices, i.e., goods made by the cheapest labour, including children, and devil take the environment too. Lotsa, lotsa stuff from sweatshops and from China.*

The owners, because Wal-Mart is still in private hands, figure prominently on the Forbes list of billionaires. Sam, the founder, died some years ago, but if you're looking for a tolerably rich Walton, you can choose Helen, Alice, Jim, John, Anne, Nancy or Robson, whose combined fortune comes to a

---

* The site where many disgruntled employees and former employees speak out <www.walmartwatch.com> provides ample testimony to the company's deplorable practices.

cool 87.5 billion dollars, or more than twice the holdings of Bill Gates, the world's richest man.[52]

Whither goest Wal-Mart, there goest also failure for unnumbered small businesses. The boarded-up for-rent shops on the main streets of smaller communities are testimony to the destructive power of the chain.

Now, harder-line Marxist friends, would you rather have the small-business federation ally with you to defeat a move to welcome Wal-Mart, because you can be quite sure they would fight like blazes, or do you want to remain pure and lose? Which is more important: your view of small business as theoretically "petty bourgeois" or the pre-accepted devastation of the living tissue of a given community? Didn't the harder-line Marxists used to say that the latter option would make them the "objective allies" of Helen, Alice, Jim, John etc., nasty capitalists all? Or am I way out of date?

A *rapport de forces* in which activists are often faced with powerful international players as well as national ones requires coalition-building. This is the only way to win. One should remember that the members of a coalition need not agree on everything in order to act together for a common purpose. Pragmatism is of the essence. Each group will naturally continue to maintain its principle focus: ecologists will remain chiefly concerned with the environment, farmers with agriculture, trade unionists with labour issues and so on. This is normal.

Candidates for inclusion in progressive alliances will vary with the circumstances but one can usually assume they will be cultural and knowledge workers (see Chapters 7 and 8), small farmers' organisations, trade unions, associations of the unemployed or of part-time workers, women's groups, students, AIDS activists, environmentalists, North-South solidarity organisations, immigrants' defence committees, human rights advocates and so on. Sometimes, depending on the issues, you should call upon consumers' rights groups, small-business federations and surely others I've forgotten – so if you belong to another group, please don't hold it against me.

Two groups which previously would have had little to do with progressive alliances are, firstly, what Americans call "faith-based" organisations and, secondly, the peace movement. These do not entirely overlap with the aforementioned participants. Long-standing peace-movement groups have traditionally had a quite different culture from that of activists in the global justice movement. When I attended the mammoth meeting of the Hague Peace Appeal in Holland, in 1999, I was astonished at the number of groups I'd never heard of or seen anywhere else.

Peace-movement participants don't automatically see any links between neo-liberal globalisation and their own issues, which are, on the whole, conflict and the arms trade; so it's up to the global justice movement to explain those links. Progressive Christians are necessarily concerned with solidarity and compassion for the poor, but they too may not always be convinced that neo-liberalism and its actors are solidarity's adversaries.

People sometimes wonder why Christian fundamentalists, of whom George Bush is the most famous, are against everything the global justice movement stands for. Although it's partly a cultural fight ("everybody knows leftists have loose morals"), I think this opposition stems more from hard-line theology. Jesus's message of "peace on earth" and "loving one another" is pretty much lost on them. Their God is mainly the Old Testament avenger (which is why they are such staunch allies of Israel); terrible in his anger.

If you know Handel's oratorio *Israel in Egypt*, the baritone aria "The Lord is a Man of War" says it all. Or take down the family Bible and read Chapter 15 of the Book of Exodus. Verse 14 says "sorrow shall take hold on the inhabitants of Palestina." If the Palestinians are suffering, it's God's will – it says so in the Bible. Tens of millions of these fundamentalists are alive, well and practicing today in the United States. The scariest among them are awaiting Armageddon, the last and decisive battle of righteousness against iniquity which they expect to come in their lifetimes. As far as one can tell, this group includes the President. Don't count on their joining any peace marches …

The social invention of the social forum

The advent of "social forums" has given a boost to coalition building. They were first given that name to distinguish them from the World Economic Forum which meets every January in Davos and in other places regionally throughout the year. At the WEF, the Masters of the Universe gather to discuss the latest phase of globalisation, their triumphs and their fears. At the social forums, activists meet to discuss how they can expose and thwart the Masters of the Universe.

Social forums are one recognition of a new political reality: no single-issue organisation can win by itself. Even so, most groups are still single-issue. Attac is not and I think this is one reason it has spread so fast and attracted so many members. The Washington Consensus is a seamless garment and all our adversaries represent one or another aspect of its doctrine. An organisation hoping to combat them effectively must know about and try to act upon all these aspects and adversaries.

Individual members of the citizen's movement will generally choose to concentrate more particularly on one or two issues. One shouldn't fall into the trap of believing one can do everything, which is a good recipe for exhaustion as well as demoralisation. For example, in Attac-France, I've "specialised" in the WTO, the GATS and to some extent Genetically Manipulated Organisms. But like all the other members, I take part in demos and actions on a variety of issues and am given a welcome opportunity to learn about questions I know less about.

Social forums are, in one sense, like Attac writ large and they began, as far as I've been able to trace, in two ways.

First, in the summer of 1999, Attac-France, then only a year old, held a ground-breaking event in the Paris suburb of Saint Denis. About 1200 people from eighty countries, including poor developing ones, attended thanks to our own funds and a grant from the Saint Denis municipal council. The programme included plenaries and workshops on different aspects of globalisation, and cultural–musical events.

Six months later we co-sponsored, with other organisations, a counter-Davos working meeting with guests from the Brazilian Landless Peoples' Movement, the Burkina Faso farmers union (present in more than 20.000 villages), the Korean Trade Union KCTU and the Worldwide March of Women which originated in Quebec.

After two days of exchanges in Zurich, we all took the train to Davos, predictably couldn't get within shouting distance of the World Economic Forum, and held a press conference after which some of us joined a ragtag band of activists in a closely contained demonstration where I have never felt so cold in my life. This is where I saw for the first time the scary Swiss police vehicles with steel grills built into their front bumpers. These slowly rise to a height of about three metres and cut off all accesses and exits the cops want to block.

The other social-forum precursor was the teach-in that took place before the Seattle demonstrations in late November 1999, organised by the International Forum on Globalisation. The IFG hired the Seattle concert hall with seating for 2400 people, and at least that many were left outside, clamouring to get in. Although this event followed a more traditional structure and was put together by a single organisation, a great many representatives of American and foreign organisations took part. In Seattle, the IFG inaugurated the tradition of holding forums plus demos on the sites of the adversary's major gatherings, demonstrating that education plus action equals the new politics. Many US organisations like Public Citizen, the Ruckus Society and a slew of others organised the core participants in the demos weeks before the event and trained them in non-violent protest methods.

The World Social Forum, held for the last three years in Porto Alegre, Brazil (2004 is in Bombay), has given rise to innumerable local, national and regional social forums. The movement has also gradually realised that we should not allow the adversary to set our calendars. When and where the Bank, the Fund, the WTO or the G-8 gather, some of us will be as well, but only some. We need our own spaces, we need to broaden our coalitions internationally and organise around common themes.

These monster forums (Porto Alegre 2003 welcomed well over 100.000 people, from 156 countries) are often chaotic but they are also energising. Like anyone else, activists need to have their batteries periodically recharged, especially because most work is going to remain local and not all of it is exciting, far from it. A problem with these forums can be that they are expensive to attend. At Attac we've set up a travel-grant scholarship system, but we haven't the money to accommodate more than ten or a dozen people. Poor, grass-roots activists who might be indispensable future partners can also be left out. It may be time to stop relying on membership fees for this purpose and go after grants and subsidies specifically targeted to including these comrades. This is a recurrent problem, one of many the movement will have to solve.

The prickly problem of political parties

Another recurrent problem we haven't resolved to anyone's total satisfaction is the relationship of the global justice movement to existing political parties. No issue so clouds the discussions among activists; no response, whatever it may be, seems so unsatisfactory to so many. The vexed question is: How should the movement relate to political parties, if at all?

The context varies from country to country but the underlying dilemma remains. Many movement activists are disaffected, disappointed ex-party members. Others may have never belonged to one and don't trust them, even the ones that are supposed to be progressive. Still others believe that part of the movement's job is to influence parties and through them the political process. Most days I tend to take this position but make no claim to having the last word. One can, however, make a few distinctions.

I think much of the wariness, the perennial distrust many global justice movement people feel with regard to political parties, stems from a fundamental misunderstanding about their nature and what they can and can't contribute to common goals. A political party is a different animal from a movement, an association or an NGO. It is differently organised because its vocation is to govern. Even small parties want to measure their political appeal and are dependent on garnering votes from the general public. They direct most of their energies and take their political positions with that end in mind.

From these banal observations flow a certain number of consequences. Parties, whether in power or in opposition, necessarily exist on the terrain of compromise. What do governing parties do, if not arbitrate and compromise between competing interests? What do opposition parties do, if not try to influence those arbitrations and compromises? The political arena in which parties operate is a place of negotiation and deal-making. This is not an insult but a statement of fact. It can also be immensely valuable. In France, social security and other aspects of the post-war welfare state were the result of a compromise between the Communist and non-Communist Left and the Gaullists, who had fought in the Resistance together.

Politics and its components – national parliaments, ministries, governments – arbitrate. A major task of the movement is to make its voice heard above the others but there is no point in expecting the government, or even the opposition, to listen to its voice alone. The movement needs to understand in a calm and analytical way that a given political party leadership is sometimes going to side with them, sometimes not.

This is why the answer to the question journalists constantly ask us – "shouldn't you become a political party?" – is so easy to answer. No, we shouldn't. We need to remain aloof and separate from the places of compromise and defend the right and the duty to weigh independently upon the decisions of parties, even and especially when they have taken power. Activists were elated when Lula won state power in Brazil, but most had no doubt that the movement should remain outside in order constantly to remind his government of its obligations. It's always a huge mistake to believe one can relax just because one's comrades have taken over the ministries.

By nature, parties must also have a position on just about everything, while movements need not because they have no pretentions to governing. At the weekly "bureau" (approximately "executive committee") meetings of Attac, we always have a large number of requests from other groups to consider: they want us to sign on for an unbelievable variety of causes. Since bad causes don't generally ask us to join their appeal for this or that, it's hard to say no, but we often do, simply because we don't have a position and to take one could divide our membership.

Here's a concrete example: in France, for all kinds of historical and political reasons which needn't concern us here, the question of civil nuclear power is divisive. I have personally been against nuclear power – civil or military – since the 1960s. Yet I think it normal that Attac not take a position on this issue, precisely because we are not, nor do we intend, to become a political party. Is this a lack of courage? That's what many opponents of nuclear power can and do say. The balance within the organisation now seems to be shifting clearly towards opposition to nuclear power and when we have a clear mandate from our local committees to change our stance, we will.

But many issues are only marginally related to our basic concerns, and they are not, to translate from a popular if slightly vulgar French expression, our onions. When in doubt, stick to your core subject. Ours is neo-liberal globalisation, its consequences for citizens worldwide and how we can fight it and eradicate the causes of its clearly harmful effects. On the other hand, national Left or centre-Left parties will need to take positions, which some movement people will approve, others not.

Just as the ecologists in your alliance or social forum are going to spend most of their time on environmental issues, women on feminist questions, students on education and so on; so parties will spend most of their time on party politics and strategy. Some will also, if you let them, try to instrumentalise you, use your organisation and its prestige for their own purposes. What's so surprising about that? These situations have to be finely judged.

For example, if you sense that a party is trying to take over a social forum or similar event for its own purposes, you can, in cooperation with the other independent organisations participating, establish a few simple rules. Ours is really simple: parties can participate in the forum so long as the organising committee agrees, but they can't participate in its organisation, choice of subjects or speakers, etc.

What about "front groups" which are parties in all but name? In the preparatory work, people have to announce who they are, who they represent, and each organisation gets only one spokesperson. Chairpersons must be tough about equal time and not allow any group to monopolise the proceedings. Messages on banners, slogans, speakers and participants in formal round-tables need to be vetted by the whole group and represent a good political cross-section.

I once saw a brilliant tactic (I didn't really object as I pretty much agreed with the slogans) in which a party brought seemingly thousands of placards and strewed them all over the roads leading to the departure point and along the beginning of the route of a major demo. Innocents who had nothing to carry picked them up and held them high throughout the entire march.

A good coup, but don't be too naive. As with other alliance partners, try always to give the benefit of the doubt unless and until proven wrong. Save your ammunition for the adversary.

To what degree can a party really be a partner? Again, it's a tough call. Here's an example. With our counterparts in Switzerland, the French movement organised a long weekend of round-tables, discussions and strategy sessions in Annemasse and Geneva – the closest we could get to the 2003 G-8 meeting in Evian. Dozens of organisations participated and the French Socialist Party (SP) asked to be able to organise a colloquium one afternoon in Annemasse. The others said fine. The Socialists asked me to speak there and, after consulting Attac whose position is basically "we'll talk to anyone except the fascists," I said OK.

Before the event was due to begin, a few hundred young people marched from one of the tent villages to the SP venue and started beating on the outside walls. Maybe they broke a window or two, but it certainly didn't qualify as a full-fledged riot and they weren't hurting people. Why this protest? Particularly since the lacklustre (and losing) presidential campaign of Lionel Jospin, there is no love lost between the independent left-of-the-Left and the SP who were the chief governing party for five years and consequently the authors of many, many mistakes and compromises. Jospin even went so far as to announce that he "was not conducting a Socialist campaign."

In other words, the SP makes a lot of people, especially younger ones, see red because they find it such a pallid shade of pink. I am myself still furious with some French Socialists because they tried to block our campaign on GATS in the European and national parliaments saying "we have to support our Commissioner, Pascal Lamy," whom I consider a card-carrying neo-liberal.

That's the scene. The apparatchiks inside the building then made the fatal mistake of calling the cops, who arrived and duly behaved as cops will, with tear gas and sticks. The SP called off the colloquium. How to judge this? On the one hand, if we want to run a democratic movement for another, democratic world, we've got to give everyone the right to freedom of expression, and the organising committee had, after all, accepted the SP presence. Undoubtedly too, a more imaginative, thought-out protest on the part of the kids would have had more impact, been far more embarrassing to the SP and not given it the opportunity to pose as a martyr which it exploited to the hilt. On the other hand, we can't be calling in the cops on each other. Heightened mutual hostility and mistrust will be the only result.

Where mistrust already exists, it can spiral and cause great damage to the movement. Let me put it this way: we can't go on punishing forever all the Socialists, Greens, radicals, Communists or whoever else messed up in your country. It's the same old question about purity. Keep them out and lose for sure or let them, or some of them, in, see how they behave, and (maybe) win. Remember why I decided to call our targets the adversary and not the enemy? Because 99 times out of 100, what we achieve is also going to be the result of a compromise.

One of our greatest problems is that it's so hard to strike a compromise or otherwise make a dent in the monolithic institutions at the international level like the Bank, the Fund, the WTO. How to get a deal? They don't have to listen to us; they're not accountable. They don't even see their longer-term interest. They defend each other. Sometimes they make a minor concession to gain time. So we can get mad, frustrated and stew in our own fury, or we can calm down and try to think coolly.

Parties, especially the larger ones, are generally not monolithic. Some of their cadres and MPs are going to be decent useful people who have irreplaceable knowledge, know how to manoeuvre expertly in their parliaments and can contribute to the movement. Just don't ask them to go beyond the bounds of what they are able to do, or to take public positions that can compromise them with their own constituencies. I don't think there is a greater proportion of corrupt or incompetent politicians than of corrupt or incompetent plumbers, doctors, or whatever. But if they are all subjected to blanket, unwavering criticism and hostility, many of the best will start saying to say to themselves, "I don't need this," and return to their former métiers.

If the national party cadres are really too distasteful, we can at least start at the local level since a good part of our politics is necessarily going to be local in any case. It's common sense to try to build good relations with the local government and local elected representatives. Try to create situations where movement members are obliged to meet and talk with people who have political responsibilities at every level, from town councillors to mayors to MPs to ministers, whether or not they share your position. Try to explain your point of view and understand theirs. The worst that can happen is that you agree to disagree. Refusing, or not seeking, dialogue is a poor tactic.*

If we call ourselves democratic, it's important to remember the dignity of the elective office and how many centuries of struggle it took for popular representation to be accepted. The disappointments politicians inflict upon us do not change that fact and representative democracy is another baby not to throw out, however murky the bathwater.

Forging alliances and dealing with political parties doesn't mean trampling on your principles or losing your credibility: it

* But see some suggestions for dialogues in Chapter 9 on illusions.

means you're serious. In our young new century, history is dealing from a new deck. We didn't choose the cards or the people across the table but we must play the hand as coolly and shrewdly as we can. And we must ardently want to win.

7

...WE COMBINE KNOWLEDGE AND POLITICS

Why is it important to understand globalisation, its actors and its impact on society and the planet, as well as the adversaries we face? Because in combination with numbers, organisation and alliances, knowledge is the basic requirement for changing the world. In this case I don't mean knowledge about a particular object or issue but knowledge as valuable in itself. Before examining other strategies for change, I want to pause and reflect on this question.

The global justice movement seems to have a disproportionate number of educators in its ranks, which is an excellent thing because teachers and academics have particularly serious responsibilities for world-changing. Though everyone is naturally invited to read it as well, I devote the chapter after this one to researchers and academics. The present one concerns knowledge in general.

As I said at the outset, politics used to be simpler. You could say "US get out of Vietnam," "stop apartheid now" or "no nukes," and, whether or not they agreed with your views, people understood instantly what you meant. They needed no specialised knowledge. Now we're confronted with an alphabet soup full of acronyms like IMF, WTO, GATS, OGM, OECD and with puzzling dry-sounding phrases from stock options to Tobin taxes. If one is unacquainted with such questions, the natural response is a yawn or a quick exit. If one can't explain them to others, the movement will not grow, it's as simple as that.

Today knowledge and political action have become inseparable. In one sense, they always have been and it's no secret that knowledge has invariably belonged primarily to the rulers – possessing it is one of the reasons they're rulers. For centuries, priests could cow the commoners (and avoid physical labour) because they had a direct line to the gods and their followers believed in their knowledge of the divine.

Maps used to be top-secret documents: they could lead you to treasure and to the best sources for slaves. They had to be kept out of the hands of your rivals. Now we use the GPS and high-resolution satellites. Because they measure the value of information, governments have always employed spies, now called by more polite names.

In the old days, a private person without at least some wealth and leisure time went through life illiterate and ignorant. Universal education changed this picture in many parts of the world (but with women still clearly at a disadvantage). Broader internet connectedness may help to democratise knowledge further but it's still useful to state the obvious: to change reality, one must first know what it is. This is not always easy and it's not encouraged by the knowledge-rich, quite the contrary because they understand that the old saying "knowledge is power" is truer than ever.

One reason the poor and powerless face such obstacles in making themselves heard is because they lack knowledge even about themselves, about the group they belong to. For example, the millions who carry the AIDS virus in Africa are each suffering singly; they have no way of saying "We, the 30 million AIDS victims ..." because most of them don't know it's a scourge of mammoth proportions striking many countries, and consequently they have no way to demand care, medicine and reparations.

Only when groups can say "we" can they form unions and defence associations. Until then they are just the workers in factory X or industry Y, the inhabitants of this or that slum or the agricultural tenants of some landlord. The Brazilian landless peasants were just separate families living in hunger until they founded the Landless Movement (Movimento sim Tierra), now 300.000 strong. Being able to say "we" reflects genuine power, and "we" in the global justice movement should respect it, use it and try to extend it to others. All of this requires knowledge.

Our adversaries have few difficulties in that regard. Governments, especially in the more developed countries, know a great deal about their populations, at least in statistical terms. They have specialised intelligence and police services, trained to deal not just with criminals, but also with the groups they see as *their* adversaries, including poor and marginal groups, the ones who were called the "dangerous classes" in the nineteenth century. Now they are also interested in us: since Seattle at least, intelligence services have opened special dossiers on movement people.

Transnational corporations know about consumers and are instantly aware of proposed laws or institutional practices that could have an impact on their business. Media corporations know about their audiences and what they can be persuaded to swallow. Top people in business and finance know long before the small shareholder when to buy and to sell. And so on.

The rich and powerful are also in a position to prevent others from learning how they became what they are and, above all, how they stay that way. To give just one example, we learned too late, and then only thanks to Greg Palast's courageous reporting, how George W. Bush became president of the United States. The Governor of Florida, who happens to be Bush's brother, called in a private firm to purge the electoral rolls of more than 57.000 legitimate voters – mostly black, mostly democrats – on the grounds that they were felons in other states who could not vote in Florida. Although Palast's research was unassailable, and although the story was front-page news in Britain and prime-time on the BBC, the US press wouldn't touch it. What citizens don't know won't hurt them.[53]

One needn't believe in conspiracies or dark plots. It's enough to recognise interests which particular groups will defend by all means at their disposal. This should come as no surprise since politics is concerned with the confrontations between such interests, whether in the local, national or international sphere. One powerful tool used to preserve one's interests is the control of knowledge. This means acquiring the capacity to present one's case forcefully through public relations, to manipulate the media and to cover one's tracks. The power to decide what can and can't be said – even thought – is the true secret weapon of the ruler.

When obliged to confront questioners, people in authority are likely to fob them off with a partial answer because they have a greater capacity for concealment than ordinary mortals. Or they may try to belittle the questioner for not knowing the dossier. A variation often invoked is: "it's more complicated than that" (whatever "it" may be). Anything can be complicated if you allow it to become so, but most of the tools of knowledge needed for action are relatively simple to acquire.

Among them are the arts of rebuttal and rejoinder, which means, yes, research and knowing one's dossier.

When the adversary is trying to intimidate you with his superior knowledge, it's important to remember that your interpretation of a given set of facts or situation is as good as his. Globalisation and the related phenomena which we've described above are not scientific concepts. This is an important distinction. If you're discussing astronomy or biology, you can assume that both you and the person facing you are dealing with established facts insofar as they can be known; backed by observation and experiment, published in reputable, peer-reviewed scientific journals and subject to revision.

With economics and other social sciences, there are no such guarantees, however much economists may try to convince us that theirs is a genuine science. Politics and ideology favouring certain systems over others always lurk just beneath the surface of the social sciences. In discussions it's often more important to determine what aspects the speakers have left out as it is to notice what they've left in.

As I'll argue in greater detail later on, even though economics can sometimes establish cause and effect, it can't claim the status of a science – or can do so only for quite trivial matters which do not affect the destiny of nations and peoples. Why is economics rarely scientific and always ideological? For one thing because the initial choice of what will be labelled a cost and what a benefit is purely arbitrary, that is, it suits the needs of a particular system or of particular interests. Costs and benefits would be quite differently classified in a different kind of economy.

Classical economics has for example absolutely no grasp of environmental matters and does not know how to record the destruction of natural capital. Cut down a forest and sell the logs, record the price you get, minus the cost of labour, amortisation of the chain saws and transport costs: you're an economist (or at least an accountant). Try to measure the cost of species destruction, silting of rivers due to soil run-offs, loss of water retention and subsequent floods, or CO_2 not absorbed by the trees: you're merely crazy, at least as seen by mainstream economists.

For them, growth is always a good thing no matter how much pollution or natural destruction it may cause. Ecologists *do* go crazy trying to get standard economists to come out of their box and face reality, so far with little success. The environment is simply forgotten. So is, usually, genuine human benefit. A new industrial process may contribute to growth, yet put thousands out of work. Or, as a dissident economist once remarked, "the quickest way to increase GDP is to have a war."

Anyone who tells you that the social sciences, like economics, sociology and political science, are objective is either lying or naive. People who practice them, including me, consciously or unconsciously base their work on values and political preferences, and their audiences have a right to know what those preferences and values are. If this disclosure doesn't occur spontaneously, the social scientist (IMF employee, etc.) should be asked pointed questions.

For example, it should surely be clear by now that one of the aims of this book is to convince you that you can develop a critical perspective on events in order to engage with others in more effective action against people and institutions I consider dangerous, not just because they represent values different from mine but also because I think I can show that their policies are needlessly harming people and frequently killing them.

My adversaries naturally want to convince you of the opposite. They will therefore include and exclude different things in their discourse. In matters of economics and politics, one should never accept arguments from authority ("it must be true because X says it is"). This is the attitude of a believer with regard to a religious institution, not that of an informed citizen.

The Italian Marxist thinker Antonio Gramsci – the one previously mentioned who spoke of "optimism of the will, pessimism of the mind" – spent years in prison, where he developed the concept of "cultural hegemony" or the cultural power that is one of the main attributes of any ruling class. Get people to think as you want them to and they will be like fish in water who aren't conscious that the medium they're swimming in is water. If you can control peoples' heads you will hold invisible power over them and need spend little time worrying about their hearts and hands.

Over the past fifty years, neo-liberals have proved themselves brilliant Gramscians whereas his lessons often seem to be lost on progressives. The Right understood early on that "ideas have consequences" (the title of a 1948 book by conservative guru Richard Weaver), and set out to fund scholars and writers, endow university chairs and research centres, pay for conferences and colloquia, serious journals and campus newspapers and generally support whoever and whatever could develop and disseminate neo-liberal ideas favorable to corporate capital, financial markets and the furthering of the interests of our present rulers. In the past twenty years, ultra-conservative US foundations have spent a billion dollars to those ends.

Consequently, their ideas are at the centre of the most powerful world institutions whether it be the United States government, the European Commission, the International Monetary Fund, the World Bank or the World Trade

Organisation. Fifty years ago, nobody except for a few cranks would have imagined that extreme, social-Darwinist ("we owe nothing to losers") views could be seriously held; nor believed that unfettered, exclusionary, environment-destroying capitalism was a viable system for any self-respecting country, much less for the world as a whole. Fifty years ago, practically everyone was a Christian democrat or a social democrat, a Keynesian (believers in public works, full-employment, New Deal-type policies) or some shade of Marxist.

That's no longer true. Many people nominally on the Left – the case of Tony Blair springs instantly to mind – are closer to right-wing leaders like George Bush than to their own political ancestors like, in Blair's case, Aneurin Bevan. No better neo-liberal than Pascal Lamy, the European Trade Commissioner and French Socialist Party member, could be imagined. Largely through the conscious efforts of the "right-wing Gramscians," the ideological balance has been slowly shifted.

KNOWLEDGE AND ACTION: THE CASE OF JUBILEE 2000

Let's look at the relationship between knowledge and political action using a concrete example which illustrates the need for mass dissemination of usable knowledge. From the late 1990s on, a powerful international campaign against Third World debt called Jubilee 2000 collected millions of signatures and held successful mass actions involving tens of thousands of people. In 1998, 70.000 of them congregated to form a human chain ("Make a chain to break the chains of debt") to tell Tony Blair's G-7 summit in Birmingham that it must act on the issue.

Jubilee went far beyond the traditional Left and brought in people who had never marched on a demo in their entire lives. I know, because I was in Birmingham and asked a lot of them.

The campaign took its name from the biblical notion of Jubilee, or periodic forgiveness of debts, and was particularly well positioned in the Church. The millennium year 2000 was to be the year the chains were broken and the debt captives set free. And this campaign did force the politicians of the G-7, the world's richest countries, to act. To general applause, they announced tens of billions of dollars worth of debt cancellations. Jubileers were jubilant and rightly proud of their achievement. They felt utterly vindicated in 1999, the year after Birmingham, when the G-7 in Cologne committed themselves to cancelling 100 billion dollars' worth of debt for forty-two countries.

But here is where the knowledge, as opposed to the undeniably important feel-good factor, comes in. In reality, relatively little debt was actually cancelled. The creditor countries played with the terminology and the press generally accepted their line uncritically. G-7 countries did, nominally, cancel some debt, yes, but this does not mean that the poorest countries were somehow to become better off. One has to examine the fine print.

First, much of the debt cancelled was debt the poor weren't paying interest on ("servicing") anyway. If a country owed, say, 10 billion, but could only scrape together the interest payments due on 5 billion, it doesn't much matter if a part of the other 5 billion is cancelled or not because the actual outlays in interest payments will stay the same.

Second, the Terrible Twins balked at cancelling any debt at all, and decided, with G-7 acquiescence, that to become eligible for relief, these countries must undergo a further three-year period of structural adjustment, later stretched out to six. Now, many years later, some have reached the "decision point," a very few the "completion point" and have received a little relief.

However, the World Bank itself has admitted that of the forty-two highly indebted poor countries – known in the jargon as the HIPCs, only four now have, in Bank-speak, "sustainable debts," twenty will still not have sustainable debts *even after* reaching the completion point, and six more are afflicted with particular problems and delays. Some, like Sudan or Somalia, are simply in limbo or have virtually dropped off the map.

For most poor countries, the mirage of genuine relief is still shimmering on the horizon. The crowning blow is that debt relief was supposed to be additional to aid, but since aid is evaporating, "in absolute terms, Highly Indebted Poor Countries are receiving less than they did in 1995" – and that is the World Bank itself speaking.[54] Indeed the situation is even worse than the Bank implies: between 1998 and 2001, sub-Saharan Africa made total net transfers of 17.5 billion dollars to the rich countries, which means they paid out in debt service and other charges 17.5 billion more than they received in development aid, grants and new loans.*

But if you haven't looked at the actual debt and total financial flows data to counter their arguments, the G-7 spokespeople are not going to do that work for you. They much prefer to deal with ignorant citizens who believe their propaganda.[55]

Jubilee 2000 had decided from the outset that it would be just what its name implied, a campaign to last only until the year 2000. So it was dissolved despite a quite limited victory. Many people, myself included, find this a tragic waste, not only because of the catastrophic ongoing damage debt causes in the South, but also because one assumes that most of the

* This figure does not include catastrophic drops in prices for their primary products, depressed because the Twins make everyone export the same small range of commodities. This benefits Nestlé and Unilever but nobody else – or have you noticed the price of coffee and chocolate plummeting at the supermarket lately?

campaign's supporters genuinely believe that they contributed to a successful effort which achieved what it set out to do and only then decided to disband.

Jubilee South, based in indebted countries like South Africa, had sharply criticised the less radical Jubilee North, and last time I heard it was still hanging on. It has held meetings in Bamako, Mali, and Guyaquil, Ecuador. But in the case of debt as in so many other cases, the South is precisely where the power is not. Creditors are not obliged to listen to the pleas of their faraway victims no matter how loudly they cry or how just their cause. Because of the disappearance of Northern campaigners who were leaning hard on creditor governments and international institutions, much political momentum has been lost. Total debt of the South is still about 2.500 billion (2.5 trillion) dollars.

THE MULTILATERAL AGREEMENT ON INVESTMENT

Here is an example of the knowledge = power equation with a happier outcome. From 1995, the MAI, or Multilateral Agreement on Investment, was being negotiated in secret at the OECD in Paris. The MAI would have given huge advantages to transnational corporations, allowing them free rein to invest wherever they wanted. The treaty's provisions laid all the obligations on states and granted all the rights and privileges to companies, including the right to sue governments for introducing measures that might limit their present or even their future profits.

Citizens' groups did not learn of these negotiations until they had already been in progress for some two and a half years. Merely obtaining the text of the draft MAI was practically a cloak-and-dagger affair. As soon as people learned what was at stake, however, they hastily cobbled together national coalitions to fight this iniquitous agreement, following what Lori Wallach of Public Citizen in the US dubbed the "Dracula strategy": if you expose the vampire to the light long enough, it will shrivel and die. The Dracula strategy requires knowledge. You must be able to describe the vampire, identify its habits and understand that its nature requires that it drink its full measure of blood. Acquiring then spreading that knowledge was essential to defeating the MAI.

Disseminating knowledge can pose problems. In France, journalists at first refused to give the MAI any space or airtime. To our dismay, their refrain was that "it's too technical, too complicated for our readers (listeners, viewers), they wouldn't be interested." Luckily for us, a couple of famous people were prepared to stick their necks out and denounce the Agreement in the press, thus giving the rest of the media permission to pick up the story. The MAI became front-page news and – surprise, surprise – people proved fully capable of understanding the implications of such a treaty once it was made available and explained to them.

After this bad publicity and some demonstrations, including a noisy one close to the OECD-MAI negotiation venue,* the French government, then a Socialist-Communist-Green coalition, was obliged to name a commission of inquiry. It invited a few members of the anti-MAI opposition to testify. Here again, it wasn't enough just to be against the Agreement. Knowledge, not just of the treaty's content, but of the international investment context, was key. Giving numbers on how few people transnational corporations actually employ and the percentage

---

* The din reportedly brought Sir Leon Brittan to the door fuming "What idiot let those hooligans use that garden?"

of their investment devoted to mergers and acquisitions (which merely increase concentration) was part of the game.

Compared to the small number of witnesses from the MAI opposition, employers unions and corporate-lobby groups were massively represented. Yet despite their testimony, over-whelmingly favorable to the MAI, the commission's final report included nearly all the opponents' arguments. Parliamentarians whom the government had never informed about the MAI began to grow angry. So much pressure was finally applied to the government that in a dramatic full parlia-mentary session Prime Minister Lionel Jospin announced French withdrawal from the negotiations.

Stopping the MAI was a case of preventing the worst. It's far more difficult to change or remove something that's already in place. Many activists want to change, or throw out, the General Agreement on Trade in Services, but changing or junking the GATS is uphill work because the text is complex and little known. People in authority like Mr Lamy, WTO spokespersons and the corporate interests they favour constantly belittle their opponents and tell the public and the media there's nothing to worry about. This is a typical knowledge battle.

We also want to introduce international taxes which would open up a whole new domain of global financial instruments for global purposes. Transnational corporations and financial-market operators can think of nothing they would like less; even concerned civil servants hesitate to rock the boat. A lot of the work of constructing another world consists in learning how to move apparently immovable objects, and having impeccable studies at one's disposal is part of the polit-ical fight.

A final point on this topic: we need detailed knowledge, yes, but only so we can then simplify it. Voltaire said: "If you want to bore people, tell them everything." A couple of hundred years later, the British economist Joan Robinson remarked that "to know anything you need to know everything. But to talk about anything you need to leave out a great deal." And I would add, "to write about anything, ditto." I'm constantly aware in these pages of the material I'm leaving out and fearful of putting too much in.

We need knowledge so that we can say true, relevant, meaningful things on a leaflet handed out in the railway station or the supermarket, explain the issue to a press journalist in half an hour, in five minutes on the radio or thirty seconds on television. Knowledge must be adapted to the medium and to the audience. Never doubt, however, that everyone can learn, with a bit of help. Learning builds confidence, it empowers and there's frankly nothing more fun than catching your adversary in a lie.

We do not have hundreds of millions of dollars like the US foundations or the corporate lobbies, but we are beginning to have the numbers and we already have the brain power and the energy. They have tried to build an impenetrable wall around knowledge so that their worldview and their institutions are never questioned. One of our most urgent tasks is to demolish that wall.

8

...EDUCATORS EDUCATE*

The many teachers and academics in the global justice movement are professional "knowledge workers" and they can play an irreplaceable role because they spend their lives trying to inspire students of all ages with the desire to learn. For the movement, these teachers and researchers are a precious resource but one which has too often been squandered.

At the Transnational Institute in Amsterdam, to which I've belonged since its founding in 1973, the fellows like to call themselves "scholar-activists." TNI has always sought to create a body of work relevant to the needs of our time. Even during the terrible political drought years of the 1980s and early 1990s when nothing one could call a movement was visible on the horizon, we still attempted to move North–South solidarity forward, using the tools of scholarship and our particular skills to analyse the structures of injustice, formulate workable

* In a somewhat different form, this chapter was my contribution to the "Critical Globalisation Studies" conference at the University of California at Santa Barbara in May 2003. My thanks to Bill Robinson and Rich Applebaum for a stimulating programme and for allowing me to publish this here as well as in their volume of the proceedings, *Towards a Critical Globalisation Studies*, forthcoming with Routledge: New York and London 2004.

proposals for change, devise the best strategies to convince our fellow citizens and decision makers of their relevance and change the *rapport de forces*.

These goals are still on our agenda, but, in contrast to the 1980s, they are now attracting innumerable cultural and knowledge workers who want to participate in this common endeavour. The other advantage over the 1980s is that there is now a genuine movement clamouring for this kind of intellectual production. Attac's popular education programme has been amazingly successful. Not only does it have a 150-member scientific council and hundreds of students of all ages in each summer university but it also produces a series of small inexpensive books, some of which sell tens of thousands of copies. We also use videos and DVDs.

In some countries, however, particularly the Anglo-Saxon ones where Attac or Attac-like movements have not taken hold, intellectuals and academics often don't know where to begin or how to go about participating in such an undertaking. They are concerned about the world, and they want to be relevant, but don't always see the connection between their disciplines and their lives as citizens.

The global justice movement has no leaders, thank God, in the sense of a cadre who give orders, but it does have individual moral and intellectual authorities who have symbolic status and are looked up to. A lot of these writers and thinkers have accompanied the movement from its inception and some were on the same terrain before it even started, so it's clear that intellectual workers *can* be relevant. Even so, the road ahead is full of potholes not to say bomb craters. So while I firmly believe in the positive role of teachers, researchers and other intellectuals in this movement, here I want to concentrate more on the risks and the mistakes they should try to avoid.

Especially in the United States, a few courageous academics are mapping out a new area called "critical globalisation studies." At the University of California at Santa Barbara, a department created only in 1999 now has 800 students majoring in the discipline. Other campuses are following suit. A lot of the subject matter of "critical globalisation studies" used to belong to the field called "critical development studies." As a long-term practitioner of the latter, I hope to be forgiven if I offer a personal answer to the question about the relevance of academia and intellectuals before trying to formulate a more general one.

My first attempt at critical development studies, though I didn't know the term at the time, was my first book, *How the Other Half Dies*.[56] Its subtitle was *The real reasons for world hunger* because it had gradually dawned on me that few were attempting to explain what those reasons were. The gap in research and analysis seemed due less to dissimulation, although there was some of that, than to subservience to an ideology that made everyone wear blinkers. The categories and concepts needed for dealing with the real reasons were simply unavailable, not part of the mental equipment of most people considered experts on the subject.

The above statements must sound insufferably smug. I can almost hear you saying, "right, all the seasoned scholars were blind, mistaken, idiots, or all three, only the rank newcomer Susan G. saw matters clearly." Point taken, but I can't approach the question of academia and intellectuals without showing my cards. So please allow me to recapitulate before explaining why I believe my judgment is not unduly harsh.

In 1973–1974 the world had just been through yet another food crisis. Famine and malnutrition were taking their usual toll in Africa and Asia and the press as well as the scholarly literature overwhelmingly offered only variations on the standard themes of drought, population pressures, low-grade technology and poor crop yields. The more adventurous might allude to government corruption, but they weren't interested in the paradox that most hungry people lived in rural areas and if they mentioned poverty it was mostly to affirm that "the poor" needed mechanisation, Green Revolution seeds and the "modernisation" that went with them.

There was virtually nothing about agribusiness or export crops, the role of food aid in changing local food habits, the Green Revolution as a negative factor or the impact of cheap imports from the Northern hemisphere on local Southern producers; there was little or nothing about land concentration and the landless, sharecropping and exploitative tenure arrangements, or outmigration from rural areas to cities. The agricultural production and policies of rich countries rarely appeared on the academic hunger horizon, doubtless because such aspects of the food picture were assumed to be positive. A statement as simple and obvious as one I made in the book – "If you want to eat, you must either have enough land to grow your own food or enough money to buy it" – was exotic in the extreme.

Who was I to say the proponents of climate/population/ low-tech explanations of hunger were wrong or biased? I was nobody. I had no credentials in the field. Not only were my academic degrees unrelated to the subject but my only extremely marginal experience was my participation in a team set up by the Washington DC Institute for Policy Studies to write a report for the World Food Conference held at the Food and Agriculture Organisation (FAO) in Rome in 1974. And even there, my role was mostly that of dogsbody.

The featured writers of the report were the recently exiled ministers of agriculture and of land reform in Allende's Chile with a supporting cast of three smart and experienced Brazilians. It was my privilege to listen to them and my job to recast the report in readable English, get it printed, get it publicised and get it there. When my luggage laden with reports and I finally made it to Rome, it was to discover that the largest delegation at the World Food Conference came from agribusiness (a.k.a., the FAO's "Industry Cooperative Programme"), immediately followed by the Americans, and that no one was talking the way the people on our team had talked.

Once home, not knowing any better, I decided to take the topic as far as I could. After a few calamities along the way and some rejections, a courageous editor at Penguin called Peter Wright took a chance on the resulting book. Everybody should have the right to one such enormous stroke of luck and this was mine.

So what's my point in the context of this chapter? Simply that it was unlikely that any genuine academic would write such a book because it approached the subject in an unorthodox way guaranteed to attract abuse and cause damage to a professorial reputation. It was even more unlikely that it should be published by a prestigious house in London rather than by a small out-of-the-way imprint with no capacity for distribution in, say, Cheltenham. This project had oblivion written all over it.

Along with Joe Collins and Frances MooreLappe's *Food First* (Joe had, like me, been part of the World Food Conference report team), neither of them academics either, *How the Other Half Dies* did initiate a new way of looking at an age-old but very contemporary problem. Widely translated, selling briskly and much appreciated by the general public (and even by the critic for the FAO magazine *Ceres*) it was icily received by most of academia.

I later got a doctorate from the Sorbonne (with a thesis concerning the transfer of the US food system to the rest of the planet[57]) because, as I continued in the field, I got sick of pompous, usually male, professors proclaiming that "this woman has no credentials for saying all the terrible things she's saying." Now I get myself announced as "Doctor" when I fear a hostile environment.

I hope a few lessons may be drawn from this story which I've inflicted upon the reader at some length. The first is that this book got around and was read because it was clear and straightforward; it eschewed a false "balance" and cautious hedging. To reach people beyond their own disciplines, academics must throw jargon to the wind, take a genuine stand and write simple, though not simplistic, prose.*

Next we must fast-forward to the basic, crassly materialist question: "Can critical scholars survive?" Progressive intellectuals rarely can – unless they are, like me, extraordinarily lucky (my late husband supported my initial efforts). The choice for most of them lies between taking a vow of poverty or academia. They will mostly teach and they will have a tough job. Whatever their field, academics are expected to transmit the

---

* An aside on prose style: I've always felt privileged to have been raised in the Episcopal Church, the American wing of the Anglican Communion, because the English divines who wrote the texts of the services and the prayer book lived during a period of splendour of the English language. The rhythm and power of it got into your ear. Although I'll never write as well as I'd like, thanks to all those Sundays I know how good writing sounds and how simplicity, clarity and grace go together. Academics who feel lost without the jargon of their trade should obtain a copy of Strunk and White's *The Elements of Style* and learn it by heart before ever again setting pen to paper or hand to keyboard. Maybe reading the *Book of Common Prayer* wouldn't hurt either.

received wisdom, are discouraged from crossing disciplinary boundaries, must frequently please their departments before pleasing themselves and for the increasingly large percentage without tenure, can't take too many risks or they will never benefit from job security. The best argument for tenure is that it creates space for critical inquiry, which is also the principle reason to deny it.

Fortunately, many still do get tenure with their creative faculties intact and their willingness to take an unconventional approach unsmothered. Whatever their status, taking risks is brave and I salute all academics who take them, particularly in a time when conformity seems more than ever demanded.*

For academics, particularly in the United States today, freedom to speak out is hedged about on all sides, and this is surely one reason why so few social scientists feel they can contribute to the global justice movement. Another is that academics may gradually acquire a vested interest in mainstream interpretations of a given reality. It becomes emotionally, professionally and often materially impossible to give up such interpretations: emotionally because the development of a worldview often coincides with a period of youth, energy and discipleship; professionally because the mainstream ensures membership in the club and consequent self-esteem; materially because, aside from one's salary, lucrative outside contracts may depend on telling the contractor what he wants to hear. A social science expert is an expert in repackaging the conventional wisdom so as to make the fewest possible enemies.

---

* A professor at a prestigious American university, now head of his department, told me how, at his tenure hearing, he was criticised for putting my book *How the Other Half Dies* on the reading list for one of his courses.

In *The Structure of Scientific Revolutions*,[58] Thomas Kuhn shows masterfully how the tenacious defence of the reigning paradigm – the mainstream explanatory consensus – rules the hard sciences. He quotes the great German physicist Max Planck to the effect that paradigms don't change because they are proved to be inadequate or wrong but because their defenders eventually die and a new paradigm can at last rise to replace the outmoded one. When he wrote that book it was far too early for Kuhn to explore the subsequent successful effort of right-wing forces in the United States and Britain to buy and pay for their own social scientists in order to develop and popularise neo-liberal ideology. In Kuhn's time, neo-liberals were still thin on the ground and their prospects at the time seemed dim.

Regardless of their near invisibility, a small covey of far-sighted, far-right forces with access to wealth did from the early 1950s create a close-knit intellectual cadre to propagate their ideas. Unlike more progressive, left-leaning foundations which would fund projects but never the production of ideas, conservative foundations based on entrepreneurial fortunes like Olin, Scaife-Mellon or Bradley did fund think-tanks. They supported the American Enterprise Institute and the Heritage Foundation in Washington, academics at the University of Chicago, the Adam Smith Institute in London and a host of other ideological producers. These "right-wing Gramscians," unlike progressives or Marxists, truly believed in the power of ideas and the concept of cultural hegemony. Now we must live with the consequences.[59]

Despite overwhelming evidence that one can, by spending huge sums, effectively buy an intellectual climate sympathetic to the most reactionary policies, the social sciences still tend to claim for themselves the supposed neutrality of the hard sciences. I'm not competent to judge whether a truly detached, objective, neutral stance can exist even in mathematics, but I'm quite sure it can't in economics, sociology or political science. Under the guise of "objective reality," one usually gets the premises and ideological framework of the reigning paradigm, which in our own time is overwhelmingly the neo-liberal worldview.

One of the prime responsibilities of critical intellectuals is to make these presuppositions explicit and this ideological framework visible, particularly for their students. They should also have the honesty to make their own stance clear. This can normally to be done by stating one's social goals and one's notion of citizenship. Unfortunately, in most lecture halls and most scholarly publications, the academic is not supposed to have social goals or to act as a citizen. These categories (like religion) are off limits and reserved for private life. This taboo serves our adversaries and is one we should collectively attempt to break.

How the academic initially frames and defines an issue is critically important. What, for example, is the point of economics? One's definition actually determines one's goals. In Karl Polanyi's sense, is the economy at the service of society? Or – as in the neo-liberal view of advanced capitalist economies – is society supposed to sit back and let the market get on with it?*

Most progressive intellectuals would, if queried, probably define the object of economic science as optimum production and distribution for the satisfaction of human needs for all members of a given community or society. The task of the economist is therefore to discover and to propose the most

---

* If you don't know it, you should read Karl Polanyi's *The Great Transformation* (Rhinehart: New York 1944). Despite its age, this is a work exceptionally relevant to our own time.

efficient methods for the collection, transformation and distribution of scarce resources so as to meet those needs, which
will include but may not be limited to clean water, adequate
food, clothing, shelter, energy and access to transport, health-
care, education, culture and particularly to "decent work" (as
the International Labour Organisation calls it). This definition,
like any other, implies value judgments. It is one starting point
for the global justice movement, and both Adam Smith and
Karl Marx, not to mention Karl Polanyi, would sympathise
with it.

Many powerful institutions, however, would not. Human
needs may even be completely absent from their worldviews
although they would be unwilling to admit it. The World Bank
rhetorically claims to uphold the "satisfaction of needs" but
rarely follows through in practice, while the International
Monetary Fund would say, if pressed, that these needs are
more likely to be satisfied by free-market, Washington
Consensus-type macroeconomic measures. The World Trade
Organisation is even more caricatural since for it, all human
activities, including food, water, health, education, culture and
life itself, are potentially profitable commodities, tradeable as
such in the world market. The Bank, the Fund and the WTO
all nonetheless profess to be concerned with "development"
(as in the WTO's misnamed "Doha Development Round").

These institutions employ vast numbers of academically
trained social scientists, particularly economists, who pretend
to be "scientific." They nonetheless consistently refuse to test
their hypotheses against objective criteria or even agree on
what those criteria should be. Under such circumstances, it is
impossible to claim the status of a hard science for economics.

We know, for example, that measured against the satisfaction of human needs, the structural adjustment policies

imposed by the World Bank and the IMF are resounding failures. Enough hindsight exists – dozens, perhaps hundreds of studies have documented the devastating impact of structural adjustment on the poor, the deterioration of health-care and education in indebted countries, the scarcity of adequate food and clean water, the mounting income inequalities. We also know that the "export or perish" policies of these same institutions have contributed hugely to drastic drops in world primary-commodity prices and, therefore, in living standards.

The "science" of economics is concerned with matters of life and death, yet provides no mechanism, no method, no check or balance which could oblige powerful economic institutions to recognise policy failure. Scientists whose experiments produce consistently negative results must eventually reject their hypotheses and change course. If a bridge collapses, the engineers who calculated the stress limits are at fault. Not so for international economics and financial institutions or their policy-making employees. They cannot be called to account for their mistakes – indeed by definition, they never make any.

Several years devoted to studying and writing about Third World debt and structural adjustment taught me the hard lesson that no level of human suffering would, in and of itself, cause their policies to change. The Bank/Fund people would instead insist that these policies were not themselves at fault; they had simply not been applied long enough or forcefully enough. Thus the economists could shift the blame for failure to the governments. This is one reason they now place universal emphasis on "governance," a term which had long been confined to business, as in "corporate governance."

I can see only two logical choices. Either one must conclude that economics as practised by major inter-governmental institutions is not concerned with human needs or, if the satisfaction of these needs is indeed the goal, then the economists who tread their corridors are hopeless at their trade. Either way, the global justice movement and critical intellectuals should devote themselves to combating them, their devastating impact on innocent human bystanders and the harmful and irresponsible social science they practice.

Positive signs nonetheless abound. As someone who spent a couple of decades fighting such institutions with a comparatively tiny band of brothers and sisters, I'm joyfully overwhelmed that thousands should now turn up in Seattle, Prague, Washington and other venues to voice their opposition to the Bank, the Fund, the WTO and the G-8 and demand that they be accountable to citizens.

Finally, I'd like to deal rapidly and in no particular order with three other aspects of the role and responsibilities of researchers, academics and intellectuals in the global justice movement.

First, let's consider the choice of subjects. Those who genuinely want to help the movement should study the rich and powerful, not the poor and powerless. This point is much better understood now than when I first wrote the same words in *How the Other Half Dies*. Although wealth and power are always in a better position to keep their secrets and hide their activities, thereby making them more difficult to study, any knowledge about them at all will be valuable to the movement. The poor and powerless already know what is wrong with their lives and those who want to help them should analyse the forces that keep them where they are. Better a sociology of the Pentagon or the Houston country club than of single mothers or inner-city gangs.

But if one is going to study the poor, it must be with them as full partners, capable of generating valuable knowledge useful to all of us. Such an approach can take time because the powerless are led to believe that their knowledge and experience are worthless and will first need to be convinced otherwise.

Second, one should use whatever methods seem to yield results or a fresh perspective, not necessarily the standard methodology of the discipline. One should also assume that just as rules are made to be broken, disciplinary boundaries are made to be crossed. This is how Fabrizio Sabelli, an anthropologist, and I approached the World Bank in *Faith and Credit*,[60] by treating the Bank as a religious institution. The fit was surprisingly close (not to mention more fun for the authors) and I hope revealing to readers.

Third, intellectuals whose goal it is to contribute to social movements have to be more rigorous than their mainstream colleagues. This is a simple rule of survival. If you're in the academic minority, you must assume that the majority will be out to get you and you'll need high-quality body-armour to be unassailable. One way to do this is to use the adversary's own words. The internet has made this technique easier than it used to be. Our foes all have sites and they are often not conscious of how their documents may sound to "normal" people. The corollary is unfortunately that the most informative documents may not be on-line – a good rule of thumb is: the smaller the intended audience of a document, the more frank and revealing the content. Leaks are best of all.

I tried to illustrate this point by inventing a fake, "leaked" document. *The Lugano Report*[61] was a "factual fiction" I wrote from start to finish but which purported to be a confidential report by an expert group to unnamed commissioners. The commissioners' question was simple: How is capitalism best preserved in the twenty-first century? The answer is not a pretty one, but only the fictional form allowed me to explore the full horror of the future if the present system prevails. I wouldn't be surprised if a genuine report of this kind exists, but if it does, it hasn't been leaked so far. (I did inform readers that the book was a hoax as I did not want it taken at face value; despite this precaution, some readers believed it anyway.)

In conclusion, it's clear that if they can avoid the pitfalls and observe a few simple rules, academics and intellectuals have much to contribute to the global justice movement. Let's remember, however, that the converse is also true – the movement can also contribute a lot to the work of academics. The growing strength and visibility of this movement is itself a rebuttal of the famous TINA doctrine ("There Is No Alternative") which the neo-liberals so desperately want people to believe. Why else would they spend so much blood and treasure constructing and disseminating their ideology?

The presence of a hundred thousand people at the World Social Forum in Porto Alegre proclaiming that "another world is possible" is surely as effective in unmasking and demolishing neo-liberalism as the critiques of a hundred intellectuals. As we analyse, criticise, propose and strategise, let's never forget that we are all part of a vast mutual liberation society, that as we work to free others, they are also working to free us.

9

...WE ABANDON CHERISHED ILLUSIONS

"The trouble with capitalism is that it's got capitalists. They're too damn greedy."

HERBERT HOOVER,
President of the United States 1928–1932

One of.the best ways to lose a battle is to base one's strategies on false premises and illusions. In thirty-some years of speaking in many countries, participating in innumerable Q and A sessions and attending meetings of campaigning groups, I've probably been exposed to more illusions than most of my contemporaries. It's trying and disagreeable to stand up and tell people that their dearly-held ideas are wrong. It seems intellectually offensive because one can never be sure. Perhaps, at last, history really is going to come up with something new. Humanly speaking, it's no fun either. People want to find the answers to the world's problems which they perceive as clearly as I do.

Call me arrogant or annoying, I still want to line up these illusions and pseudo-solutions against the wall and open fire.

I've met these well-meaning notions time and again and they deserve to be shot, not because they're violent criminals – they're usually rather meek and mild – but because they're time-wasters and morale-sappers. Worst of all, they let the adversary get on with his dirty business while we dither or look off into the middle distance, in the wrong direction.

Here are my prime candidates for the firing squad.

ENOUGH IS ENOUGH

A common thread in the fabric of illusions is some peoples' belief that somehow "they," the rich and powerful, can be brought to share our views and genuinely agree to renounce their wealth and power. I respect the moral imagination of such people ("no one can possibly be that greedy; at some point everyone has to cross a certain threshold labelled 'enough'") but I cannot agree with their analysis. I willingly concede that there's the occasional Cincinnatus, the noble Roman general who prefers his plough and his farm to palaces and power, but when we're talking about an entire class, not just the rare individual, this is *never* the case.*

Listen rather to Michael Parenti who says, "there's only one thing this class has ever wanted throughout the whole of

---

* French readers may object that the "night of August 4th 1789," when French aristocrats and clergy renounced their feudal privileges, disproves my claim. However, as Jean-Paul Marat wrote at the time in *L'Ami du Peuple*, what they called their "sacrifices" were also an attempt to sidetrack the proceedings of the National Assembly into endless discussions about the legal consequences of the abolition of privileges and to prevent discussion of the *Declaration of the Rights of Man and the Citizen* and above all "the great work of the Constitution." Marat's amazingly perceptive political article was too much even for the Revolutionary press. Written and refused publication on 6 August, it did not appear until 21 September 1789.

history and that's everything." Recall the Walton clan with their collective 87 billion dollars and their employees living on food stamps. I have no doubt that this class would, given half a chance, drag us all blithely back to the nineteenth century. From now on, let's call the rich and powerful the R and Ps for short. I include in this category the institutions, public and private, that serve them – the ones we met in the chapter on actors.

I'm sorry to say that the concept of enough is not part of their theoretical vocabulary or practical baggage. The lower limits to human existence – destitution, hopelessness, exclusion – are clearly defined, but no upper limits have yet been set, at least not in any capitalist society. It would save us an enormous amount of time, argument and grief if everyone could just accept the simple assertion that for the R and Ps, nothing will ever be "enough."

The corollary to this observation is that they are not swayed by rational argument. Thus a modest tax on financial transactions is "totally feasible and totally unacceptable." We have excellent cogent arguments on our side. Because they know this, our adversaries are often reduced to explaining that the richer and more powerful they themselves become, the more benefits they will be able to shower upon a grateful world. This is obviously rubbish, but it's also the homage vice pays to virtue. Right-wing governments' tax cuts for the best-off individuals and for corporate welfare are always defended on such grounds.

THERE'S NO TOMORROW

A slightly more problematic illusion that's easier to agree on is this: these people must somehow recognise their own longer-term interests. It's incredible, it brings you up short, but in fact they almost never do. As I argued in The *Lugano Report*, Franklin Roosevelt with his New Deal was the saviour of American capitalism, yet the very people he was struggling to save loathed him and refused to say his name, particularly in the presence of women and children, calling him instead "that man."

"Short-term" is alas the name of their game. In recent times, only World War II seems to have broken this mould and forced the Establishment to look further down the road, notably with the creation of the World Bank and the IMF, progressive institutions at the time, as well as the Marshall Plan for the reconstruction of Europe which cost nearly three percent of the US Gross Domestic Product and was worth every penny.

COME LET US REASON TOGETHER ...

The fact that R and Ps do not generally recognise their own longer-term interest is one reason why "dialogues" must be handled with care. In nearly all cases, the benefits of dialogue with one's adversaries are strictly limited. One doesn't want to appear closed-minded or disdainful, so one accepts their invitations to engage in such exchanges. You can go and talk to the World Bank and business associations if you like, you might learn something and I do it myself in certain cases, but you should not believe that your arguments will persuade them nor that you can convince them that their own interest would be to adopt more forward-looking policies.

Institutions frequently confuse "dialogue" with "explanation." Since they cannot conceivably be mistaken or unjust, they assume that if you disagree with their position, the problem must be either bad faith or faulty communications.

They haven't explained well enough. OK, they think, some of the people against us are just troublemakers or politically motivated, but we can convince the others through "dialogue" and then they'll shut up.

These institutions seldom recognise common usage, which defines a "dialogue" as taking place between equals. They are more interested in monologues and public-relations exercises directed from top to bottom. This attitude explains why, for example, few non-governmental organisations (NGOs) still bother to attend the "dialogues with civil society" held by the Trade Directorate of the European Commission. One or two NGOs go in order to brief the others, but otherwise these sessions serve only to justify the Commission's pre-defined positions.

The adversary may invite you so that you serve as his "progressive alibi." "See how tolerant and broad-minded we are! We have actually invited the notorious anti-globalisation movement's X or Y." So long as you know that's what's going on (maybe even say so from the floor) there's no harm in going, particularly when it's a one-off event.

A different case is when the adversary invites you to a prolonged dialogue to gain time, or worse still invites a "permanent dialogue." Sadly but predictably, some moderate NGOs can be counted on to cooperate and let it stretch out forever, apparently hoping that someday the dawn will break and a 180-degree turn in policy will ensue.

As an example, recall the story about the defeat of the Multilateral Agreement on Investment. In October 1998, the French government announced its withdrawal from the MAI negotiations, some smaller countries like Belgium followed and from then on the deal was clearly off. But the OECD, where the MAI had been negotiated since 1995, refused to admit defeat. At the beginning of December, just before the MAI cadaver was to be formally interred, it sent out a carefully worded invitation to hold a dialogue about this defunct treaty and the OECD's own future role in crafting investment rules. Two major international NGOs, which I shall not name to save them embarrassment, actually accepted. But some of us remember who they were ...

Corporations and their front groups will often try to shield themselves with some big NGO names. Recall the Global Compact at the United Nations, the project conceived by Kofi Annan with the help of the ex-chair of Nestlé, Helmut Maucher. To join the Global Compact, all a transnational corporation need do is sign on to nine principles in the areas of labour, human rights and the environment. It will not be monitored because the UN has no capacity to do so; the company gets a free ride.

The UN asked some prominent NGOs as well as the International Confederation of Free Trade Unions (ICFTU) to sign on to the Global Compact where, as many of us see it, their role is clearly to serve as moral guarantors. Now it seems Amnesty for one is having second thoughts, and a good thing too. The best way not to be tainted by proximity is to refrain from associating too closely, especially in permanent arrangements, with neighbours whose behaviour one has no hopes of monitoring much less controlling.

Dialogue is all very well, and one shouldn't neglect the possibility of a tactical breakthrough, but like anything else it reflects power relations and requires setting objectives and/or conditions. For example: "We will recognise that you – corporation A or institution B – are meeting us in good faith if you do X by date Y." If these objectives are not met within a reasonable time, that is the time to pack up one's briefcase and return to more fruitful labours. It is up to the corporations or the institution to change – not the NGOs. The latter should therefore know exactly what they want to obtain before entering into any arrangements which can use them as cover.

THE SLIPPERY PRONOUN

Who, then, can stand up to "them," the public or private R and Ps? Across the table, across the battlefield from them, is that slippery, all-purpose pronoun "we." I've been using "we" all along, but now it's time for the critique. This pronoun's job is all too often to pretend that there's basically just one big happy human family made up of basically decent people with basically similar interests. If only "we" all did A, B and C, hunger and misery would disappear, wealth would be shared, every child would inherit a place in the sun, another world would, in fact, be possible. This belief is basically wrong.

In every circumstance, at every historical moment, one has to have a clear notion of who the pronoun "we" includes. The "we" will vary with time and with shifting alliances and should be carefully assessed before one even tries to wring any concessions from the adversary because the R and Ps do not and cannot share similar interests with the groups proposing change and thus challenging their interests. This is called evaluating the *rapport de forces*; the balance of forces. The adversary will be obliged to notice, respect and engage with you when the "we" is sufficiently numerous and determined, not before.

JUST ADD WATER ...

Another illusion is that of the efficacy of the ready-made formula for change. This is nothing new. The nineteenth-century reformer and utopian Robert Owen seriously proposed "a world convention to emancipate the human race from ignorance, poverty, division, sin and misery." Although they do not generally concern sin, I receive cart-loads of these proposals through the post or over the internet; eager souls anxious to have their ideas recognised press their pamphlets upon me as I head out of lecture halls.

I know well the urge to solve the world's problems at a stroke and am not above committing this sort of document myself. I did so right after September 11 in a piece called "Clusters of Crisis and a Planetary Contract."[62] My only excuse is that I perceived a remote chance in the wake of the terrorist atrocities that Western powers might for once recognise their own interests and radically change course. I was naive.

All these powdered solutions – just add water – are best described in French. They "assume that the problem has already been solved" ("supposer le problème résolu"). In other words, they're the result of faulty logic as well as faulty politics. Indeed, *if* the R and Ps were collectively willing to renounce their privileges, which include running the economy, politics and society for their own benefit, *then* some of these schemes would indubitably work. But they haven't a prayer of being acted upon *until* that precondition is met, meaning, generally speaking, never.

Furthermore, any blanket solution relevant to the problems at hand would necessarily require redistribution of wealth and power. If it were to come close to being adopted, an unlikely development, it would instantly provoke the hostility of the R and Ps who would mobilise their counter-attack faster than you can say "Davos." Those who propose these instant schemes assume the problem already solved when they ignore this hostility. Since they are usually quite nice people themselves and unwilling to harm anyone, they disregard the forces capital is prepared to deploy in order to beat back genuine solutions.

To provide just one, almost trivial, example (though far from trivial for the people whose lives are at stake), cash sales for the US pharmaceutical industry in sub-Saharan Africa are negligible, yet these companies are prepared to stonewall all reforms to prevent generic AIDS drugs from reaching the poorest patients.*

They claim that allowing generic drugs for AIDS, tuberculosis and malaria would allow the do-gooders to get a foot in the door, that other diseases would soon be added to the list, that countries like South Africa capable of producing such drugs would export them not just to poor neighbours but back to the rich countries, and so on. The arguments are endless, but they come down to the simple statement that everything and every place belongs to the market. The size and value of that market are not the point.

Other instant solutions are harmless. Some may be beneficial, right now, to some limited groups of people. I am all for them; far be it from me to oppose anything that can alleviate anyone's daily burden. People *should* engage in devising practical solutions to local problems, they *should* act wherever they are on whatever issue they can tackle. Argentineans should invent their own currencies, and workers manage their bankrupt factories. Taking such actions to their logical conclusions can also be uniquely pedagogical, so please believe me when I say I support them wholeheartedly.

This stance is, however, quite different from being convinced that these actions, added together, can at some future

---

* An inadequate compromise was reached in August 2003, just before the WTO ministerial meeting in Cancún.

date cover the whole planet or substantially change existing patterns of income or power distribution. My reasons are the same as those cited above: if such schemes showed signs of spreading their reach beyond fairly marginal groups and exceptional circumstances, the R and Ps would instantly oppose them, if necessary by force.

This is why I believe that for the foreseeable future, currencies will continue to be issued by Central Banks, not by Local Exchange Trading Systems (LETS); most vehicles will continue to run on whatever fuel (perhaps other than petroleum) is distributed most widely by mammoth corporations, not on sunflower oil; most coffee and tea consumed in the North will not be "fair trade" products but the usual standard brand names packaged by TNCs.

This does not mean, however, that one must acquiesce to the power of capital. It does mean that most politics involves seizing opportunities and making spaces, however small, and exploiting them to the hilt so that genuine politics, in the broadest sense, can begin to happen. Anti-capitalism, to me, means seizing the opportunities and participating in making these spaces, through whatever means are at hand. The rest we cannot foresee.

I'M A GUILTY CONSUMER

More pervasive and more pernicious among illusions to be fought is the assertion that "If we [there goes that pronoun again] all just changed our consumption habits and made different individual choices, then transnational corporations would also be obliged to change." This approach seems reasonable, even market-based. It's also mildly masochistic and one hears it a lot: "it's my fault." It's the fault of all of us because "we" are all guilty consumers.

Nonsense. If you are a confirmed masochist, go ahead and believe that it's your fault but I can assure you it's not mine. We are all embedded in a capitalist society. Assuming that one can escape from it through consistently practising alternative consumption is optimistic to the point of folly.

Once more, I have nothing against – indeed I encourage – ethical consumption. It's definitely good to make sure that as many products as possible have been produced with as little human and natural exploitation as possible. The fair-trade movement is an admirable vehicle for such change and farmers producing honest food anywhere are to be treasured and supported. But the bulk of everyone's consumption? In your dreams.

In my first book *How the Other Half Dies*, I referred to this mistaken belief, in a slightly different guise, as the "one less hamburger" school. It was a popular myth of the time to affirm that "if we all ate just one less hamburger a day/week," this would somehow divert grain presently used to feed livestock for the direct consumption of poor people. Because one-less-hamburger enthusiasts posited some sort of direct conduit between the overfed with a meat-rich diet and the underfed in the South, some well-meaning people thought they ought to become vegetarians, not to enhance their well-being or to conform to their ethical principals but because if "we" all did this, the poor would somehow be fed.

Sorry to play Cassandra again and say "rubbish," but the fact remains that, in the wildly unlikely case that demand for meat were seriously reduced, the only thing that would happen is that the supply of meat would diminish. Fewer cattle would be raised, less feed-corn planted. The "savings" would not be distributed to the hungry. The problem of hunger concerns poor people and it is the result, in one sentence, of their lack of land to grow food or of money to buy it. It's the same old wealth-and-power refrain.

Even if reducing meat consumption (or some other kind of consumption) were the solution, I'm afraid one could still never convince the majority of hamburger-lovers to give them up, at least not so long as they can afford meat. Statistically speaking, any society that becomes slightly better off always increases consumption of two items: meat and energy.

But leave this universal fact aside as well: as Justin Podur has remarked, "the everyday consumption of the people in the rich countries is an outcome of the system, not the cause." "People in poor countries aren't starving because the people in rich countries are consuming," he continues, "but [because] people in both regions are being used by a system that cares nothing about them." Here's the clincher: "If history judges us who live in the rich countries harshly, it won't be for our individual consumption choices but for not fighting the structures of domination and power relations that set the context for those choices...." Well said.[63]

The only consumer behaviour corporations take into account is organised by marketing and shaped by advertising. Changes individuals might make in their lifestyles, even if there are many individuals and many changes, will not register because these companies are simply too huge. Yes, a well-explained mass consumer boycott can be an entirely different matter and it can have an impact, but such tactics can't be attempted too often as the corporate offence must also be large, visible and easily illustrated. Gauging the numbers of probable followers is important before trying to launch such a boycott or it can even backfire by demonstrating the movement's weaknesses.

Naming and shaming are powerful tools when they are used collectively, and there's perhaps nothing the companies fear more than well-directed blows against their reputations and especially their brands. Boycotts against South-African Outspan oranges or against Shell for its life-destroying actions against the Ogoni people in Nigeria and its drilling for North Sea oil were media successes. They contributed to the end of apartheid and to justifiably besmirching Shell's reputation.

But such efforts take dynamic and imaginative organisation and are a far cry from wishful-thinking, individual lifestyle or consumption changes. Make those individual changes if they make you feel better and healthier, but don't allow them to make you feel virtuous with regard to the world at large. And please don't expect the rest of us to applaud: we have more important things to do.

10

...WE PRACTISE NON-VIOLENCE

Is it legitimate to confront one's adversary with violence? The answer the global justice movement collectively brings to this question is crucial for its future. As many people in the movement know, my personal position is one of unequivocal opposition to any kind of street violence accompanying movement demonstrations. Here I want to explain my reasons.

The question of the efficacy and legitimacy of violence in response to repression has been central to modern political movements at least since the American and the French Revolutions. The Boston Tea Party of 1775 protested unjust taxation with a political "happening." American colonists dressed as Indians dumped 373 chests of British tea worth 75.000 pounds sterling – a king's ransom at the time – into the Boston harbour. This act of violence against property was applauded by the colonists from Maine to Georgia, and the British Crown predictably responded with escalating repression which in turn led to the Declaration of Independence and the launching of the Revolutionary War.

From the French Revolution to the Russian one and beyond, we need hardly review the literature of the past two centuries, but we do need to remember that the debate concerning the relationship between politics and violence has had a long history, especially when state power was at stake.

Let us try to summarise our own situation. We are entering a new historical phase marked by organised international opposition to neo-liberal capitalist globalisation, itself characterised by the dominance of giant transnational corporations and financial markets in which the accumulation of power and profit are the goals, in which market values take precedence over human ones. All human activities are transformed into commodities. International institutions like the World Bank, the IMF, the World Trade Organisation, and the European Commission, along with many private institutions, serve to implement the neo-liberal programme which results in escalating inequalities, exclusion and all too often death.

The movement's problem is to determine whether, if at all, these adversaries and these ills can be opposed through violence. Since the sobering impact of the events that occurred during the demonstrations in Göteborg and Genoa in June and July 2001, and the terrorist attacks on September 11 of the same year, there are signs that nearly everyone in the movement will now refuse to tolerate violence in our ranks. I hope so, but that may not be enough and the new phase poses its own specific problems.

Let's start from the event when the issue first came to the fore. Most commentators date popular opposition to globalisation from the World Trade Organisation's ministerial meeting in Seattle (November–December 1999) which ended in fiasco for the WTO. The tens of thousands of demonstrators in Seattle were overwhelmingly non-violent. A great many had undergone training in the techniques of non-violent protest and they were extraordinarily brave, "locking down" and facing tear gas and beatings but refusing to move.

The media, as usual, had little to say about these thousands; they stressed rather the actions of a few dozen muscular young men in black who broke windows, trashed shops and set fires in rubbish bins. These young men were followed later that same night by the inhabitants of the poorer Seattle neighbourhoods who had not participated in the demonstration but swarmed into the city centre to take advantage of the confusion and help themselves to the free merchandise on offer.

Later demonstrations in Europe led to much more serious incidents. In Göteborg, Sweden, police used horses and dogs against protestors (having promised the organisers they would refrain from using such methods) and three young demonstrators were shot with real ammunition. One was seriously wounded; he has fortunately since recovered. A month later, at the G-8 counter-summit in Genoa, the police again opened fire with live bullets, this time killing Carlo Giuliani.

The Italian police subsequently raided a school where activists were sleeping. They hunted down, kicked and clubbed people who offered no resistance. At least 100 people were seriously injured but even today we do not know all the details because the formal inquiry promised by the Berlusconi government into this shameful display of police brutality has, unsurprisingly, never been undertaken. The results of private commissions of inquiry are not yet available but there are films that show the extent to which the police were out of control, or perhaps merely following orders.

These are, very briefly, the events to which most ordinary people and journalists refer when they speak about the "violence of the anti-globalisation movement." In Scandinavia, this issue continued to dominate press coverage and to incapacitate the whole movement for well over a year after Göteborg. Although in 2003, the Scandinavian movement seemed gradually to be recovering its dynamism, permanent scars may remain because such clashes were previously unheard of and culturally off limits in these societies.

In contrast, there was no violence at all in Washington for the World Bank–IMF demonstrations in April 2000, in Barcelona in June 2001 and in March 2002, nor at the huge European Social Forum demonstration in Florence in November 2002. The sight of a million people marching there for democracy and peace was especially gratifying because the rabble-rousing journalist Oriana Fallaci had predicted mayhem (she hoped!) and warned Florentine shopkeepers and residents to shutter their windows and stay barricaded at home.

We first need to distinguish between violence against people and violence against property. For example, I personally condemn violence against people, whether it comes from an unjust economic system, from the state, from terrorists or from protestors, and I condemn it for moral reasons. Killing innocent people at work, as in the World Trade Center, or people who were simply in the wrong place at the wrong time, or, like the Basque terrorists, targeting elected officials and civil servants, or using real bullets against protestors, is despicable and unacceptable. Murder is murder, whoever commits it.

Violence against people is only justified if it is used in genuine self-defence or to save lives and thereby reduce the overall level of violence. Killing Hitler at an early stage would have been, for example, an excellent idea. This doesn't mean, however, that one should take the liberty deliberately to taunt the police and provoke their violence so as to escalate the conflict and thereby "justify" using violence in self-defence.

One must also distinguish contexts in which violence against people can be considered legitimate. When a country is occupied by a foreign power, resistance of whatever nature is legitimate. In a totalitarian state, with no recourse or legal mechanisms for redressing grievances, violence may also be justified, but that doesn't necessarily make it wise. In Soviet-ruled totalitarian Czechoslovakia activists like Václav Havel and his comrades refused to employ violence and won their velvet revolution. In democratic contexts, however flawed, which guarantee freedom of speech and of the press as well as an independent judiciary, violence against people shouldn't be an option.

What then about violence against property during mass demonstrations? Here my argument is rather a tactical one. It doesn't pay. It is a disservice to the goals one is presumably fighting for; and it's counter-productive especially when committed against small shops and ordinary people's cars. Smashing bank windows may provide useful business for glass merchants but has no effect whatsoever on transnational capital, not even symbolically. I therefore condemn such violence on political, practical and tactical grounds.

Still I believe that violence against property is also sometimes justified, when all democratic means of redress have been exhausted. Some celebrated cases include the dismantling of a McDonald's restaurant under construction in southern France by José Bové and his comrades, or the uprooting of genetically manipulated crops growing in open fields. These I see as more reminiscent of Boston Tea Party-type actions, with corporations or the WTO playing the role of King George.

Most people have forgotten that the McDonald's episode was a protest against the decision of the World Trade Organisation which authorised US sanctions to the tune of 116 million dollars against European goods in retaliation for the European refusal to import hormone-injected beef. One of the products on which the US slapped punitive tariffs was

Roquefort cheese. Through no fault of their own, Bové and his fellow sheep farmers in a poor area of France suddenly lost a significant slice of their market and their livelihoods, with no democratic recourse to obtain redress of their grievances.

A legal system which condemns sheep farmers to suffer for a decision taken long ago and far away by others – even if the European decision to refuse hormone-fed beef was right – is bizarre and indefensible in any legal system or customary law I've ever heard of. Why should they be punished for a "crime" they had nothing to do with?

I once participated myself in an action to uproot GM rapeseed because I believe that the dangers to the environment and the dangers of total corporate takeover of our food supply far outweigh the loss to the company using the experimental field. The crime of *non assistance à personne en danger* – "refusing help to a person in danger" – exists in French law. Allowing GM crops to pollute the environment in my view constitutes *non assistance à société en danger*. I'd do it again if asked.

THE VIOLENCE OF THE STRONG

Some movement participants feel that any tactics are justified by the level of structural violence in the world, that anything "we" may do will be utterly insignificant compared to the violence committed by the world economic and political system. They have a point.

If murder is murder, then allowing needless deaths to occur from poverty and hunger in the midst of plenty is despicable and unacceptable as well. Aren't the conditions of life for half the world violent? If a thousand children die somewhere every day from preventable diseases, if a third of all children die before the age of five, as in Angola, isn't that violence against the children and their families? If the environment becomes so damaged or the land so degraded that people can no longer eke out a livelihood, doesn't violence against nature also qualify as violence against human beings who depend on nature? Are people slowly dying of AIDS not suffering violence when drugs exist which could help them to live more normally? Are women and children working twelve hours a day in sweatshops with no rights whatsoever not being treated violently? Examples abound.

Protestors in the movement are convinced – and I agree – that inter-governmental organisations like the IMF and the Bank are guilty of structural violence, sometimes directly through livelihood-destroying projects, sometimes in the longer term by creating policy frameworks in which violence intensifies.

The burden of debt in the South is a textbook example of how violence is done to countless millions of innocent citizens. Debt gives the IMF and the Bank enormous power and their Structural Adjustment Programmes are the epitome of violence, sometimes directly provoking it. When the prices of basic goods, vital for survival, like bread, rice, water, cooking oil, or fuel are doubled or tripled, people take to the streets. These "IMF riots," as those who take part call them, have occurred in dozens of countries. They have caused hundreds of deaths, injuries and imprisonments – but where does the violence really come from? From the people protesting or from the institutions that have imposed impossible sacrifices on them?

Two people I should particularly like to see tried by an international criminal tribunal are first, for obvious reasons, Henry Kissinger, second, Michel Camdessus, who blandly oversaw the application of the Fund's death-dealing policies for thirteen years (and now sits on the Vatican's Justice and Peace Commission).

Movement people also frequently see their own governments in the North as accomplices to violence in the South because they are the principle supporters and contributors to these international institutions. A growing distrust of virtually all political leadership is an increasingly prominent feature of the protest movement, and this is, in many ways, a worrisome development for the future of politics itself.

BE ANGRY BUT BE SMART

In my experience, many people today, especially young people, are spontaneously internationalist. They are genuinely concerned not just by their private lives and the politics of their own countries but about what is happening half-way around the world. They feel angry, personally offended, when their governments, the members of the European Union or of the G-8, meet in circumstances of revolting opulence as if they had the right to rule the world, only to produce ridiculously feeble communiqués almost never followed by concrete results.

Take the luxurious Genoa mountain which gave birth to a debilitated, anemic mouse: in 2001 the G-7 promised to raise a billion and a half dollars to combat AIDS, malaria and tuberculosis, whereas only weeks before Kofi Annan had asked for 7 to 10 billion dollars to fight AIDS alone. Then the G-8 governments didn't even follow through on their meagre promise. George Bush was again making promises in Africa in the summer of 2003. The same lot of politicians has been falsely pledging genuine debt relief for years. The G-8 in Evian, France, in 2003, went through the same motions and mouthed the same noble sentiments.

One could cite dozens of instances of structural violence inherent in a world of dismaying inequalities constantly overlooked by these prestigious politicians and the media. People are justifiably fed up with the lack of seriousness on the part of a leadership which doesn't lead or takes the wrong direction. It's easy to be furious with them and want to smash something or punch somebody, and since the heads of the G-8, the Fund, etc., aren't available, well ...

THE MONOPOLY OF LEGITIMATE VIOLENCE

The question, however, remains: is it wise or effective to confront "their" structural violence with violent demonstrations? The German sociologist Max Weber famously defined the state by its "monopoly of legitimate violence." In other words, they have the police, the attack dogs, the guns, the army, the courts and the prisons. They also have, on the whole, impunity. If you kill a policeman, under any circumstances, including self-defence, you may well spend the rest of your days in jail. If a policeman kills you, even if you were committing no crime at the time, it is likely that your family will have no recourse and will receive no compensation.

If violent state actors are called the army and the police, violent non-state actors are called terrorists. They generally claim to be carrying out their actions in the name of some higher principle, often that of liberation or of ridding their corner of the world of whatever ghastly regime is in power there. Some of them subsequently become prime ministers – look at Israel.

The terrorist attacks of September 11 left the world in a state of shock. Some people have said that an assault on poverty and exclusion could eliminate such horrible actions. It's tempting to believe this, but in the case of Al Qaida, I doubt it. From what we know, the perpetrators of these acts were educated, middle- to upper-class Arabs, mostly Saudis and Yemenis, who took no interest whatever in the poor people of their own societies nor even in the plight of the Palestinians.

It's true that poverty and exclusion breed resentment which breeds violence which – particularly if it is combined with some form of millennial or fundamentalist religion – can and will strike anywhere. We have a duty to reduce the conditions that foster hatred, but we shouldn't believe that violence will then be altogether eliminated.

The actions of Al Qaida against innocent victims can in no way be justified. This is also the case for the United States which has shown little compassion for innocent civilians (sorry, I meant "collateral damage") in other countries. Without going as far back as Indo-China, or as far forward as Iraq, we know that US bombing, military campaigns and sponsored *coups d'état* have caused innumerable civilian casualties in dozens of countries.

Everyone knows too that the United States practically invented the Taliban and supported Bin Laden after the over-throw of the Soviet-backed regime in Afghanistan in 1992, just as they had previously supported Saddam Hussein. Even the wars America doesn't fight itself are frequently fought with American-manufactured weapons. What can be said of the unwavering American support for Israel no matter what its policies? What excuse is there for fifty years of training thou-sands of future Latin American torturers and death squads at the School of the Americas in Fort Benning, Georgia?

Who do you think said the following: "Let us get on with the business of killing our enemies as quickly as we can and as ruthlessly as we must." Bin Laden? No, former presidential candidate and Republican Senator John McCain in the *Wall*

Street Journal, exhorting the Bush government to escalate the war in Afghanistan. It's tragically clear that other civilian lives are nowhere near as important as American lives. The global peace movement is often accused in Europe of being anti-American. This is false: Americans are themselves a vitally important part of it. We do justifiably criticise the US government and whatever countries choose to follow a unilateralist American leadership along whatever violent path it chooses.

I can't evoke the war against Iraq because it would require a whole other book. It revealed the chilling option for violence and war which is now integral to Bush-administration policy, even if it cannot carry out another full-scale war immediately.

MOVEMENT RESPONSES

After this recapitulation of "their" violence, let me turn to "ours." I say "ours" because I participate in the movement, my convictions are tied to my politics, and I believe it would be naive and foolish to claim that violence in our own ranks no longer poses any threat. It does and it will, if only because "they" will try to incite us to practise violence because it is dangerous – not for those against whom it is directed, but for ourselves and the goals we profess to defend.

I argue that the people on our side who engage in violence are not just misguided but are actively working against the rest of the movement and the aims they claim to support. Here are some reasons why:

• Violence directs the media and therefore the public away from the message of ninety-nine percent of the movement and attracts attention only to the actions of a tiny minority. Our arguments do not come across.

Thus in Göteborg, the long debate on a giant outdoor screen between seven representatives of the protestors (including myself) and Romano Prodi, Javier Solana, Joschka Fischer and the Swedish and Portuguese prime ministers was not reported by the media at all. Nor were the many debates, forums and peaceful actions that preceded the demonstrations.

The same happened in Genoa where the Genoa Social Forum, made up of about 700 Italian organisations, organised innumerable discussions on a broad variety of issues where participants explained and discussed their goals and positions non-stop. After that, we hear our adversaries repeating "You have nothing to propose" when we have just spent days making proposals. Yet we cannot draw the world's attention to them because it's riveted by the media on the violent actions of a few individuals who, indeed, propose nothing at all.

When 80.000 people converged on the border between Switzerland and France to protest the G-8 of 2003, the *New York Times* told its readers how a few brats trashed a BP gas station. Period. This was the only "incident" during the entire march and the only thing reported by the US "newspaper of record."

- Violence in mass demonstrations is anti-democratic. If we want a democratic world then we must first try to run a democratic movement.

The preparations for Göteborg involved about 350 different Swedish groups; twice as many for Genoa; dozens in France, etc. Through long, often frustrating discussions, a process of give and take, and learning to work together, these coalitions, painfully but democratically, arrived at a consensus. Yet they are held in contempt by the so-called "Black Bloc" and less well-organised violent elements. They turn up at the last moment with their own individualistic, selfish and self-indulgent agenda. Some of them are "skins" (fascists), who are in contact and turn up from all over Europe anxious to discredit the progressives.

Sometimes, as in Geneva in June 2003, such people are a kind of minority subculture, like the black-leather heavy-metal spiky-haired and grubby people from Zurich whose only goal in life is apparently to break things. One would have to ask a qualified psychologist or anthropologist if they have any interest in politics at all.

Another group of "last minute people" does claim to act from political motives. In their view, everyone but themselves is a "sleepwalker" (the term used on one of their websites) in need of awakening. The best way to give the rest of us a jolt is by revealing, through provocation, the true, repressive nature of the state. Although this repressive nature may not exactly be news, one has no choice, as the "revelation" is imposed by behaviour which is dictatorial, macho and contrary to our collective choices. It reminds me of the old arguments for the revolutionary party which "sees more clearly" than everyone else and must consequently take over the direction of the ignorant masses. No thanks: been there, done that – or rather, had that done to us.

- Violent groups are usually dressed alike and masked and are thus easily infiltrated by police and fascist elements.

This is the oldest trick in the world and we have observed it in our own demonstrations time and again. Sometimes the black-clad masked cops are so unobtrusive they can be seen getting in and out of their police vans. They try to infiltrate protests for the excellent reason that they can then give governments a perfect excuse to criminalise and crack down on everyone, no matter how peaceful.

• It is not terribly intelligent, tactically speaking, to confront the state where it is strongest, on the terrain of its "monopoly of legitimate violence."

A good battlefield commander tries to exploit the adversary's weaknesses, not lead to his strengths. Taking a few metres of pavement here or there is not a strategic objective. It can be seen, rather, as adolescent egocentrism and bravado. It opens no political spaces and means nothing for the future.

I have been saddened and astounded to read individual narratives found on some sites close to the Black Bloc and think the writers must be very young and/or very insecure. Definitely members of the "take a few metres of pavement" school, they stress "how powerful doing such and such an action made me feel." Frankly, who cares? Seeking a fleeting thrill of empowerment is childish. We're trying to run a political movement here, not group therapy.

• Violence discourages many people from participating in mass mobilisations.

We want to build a broad-based, inclusive, trans-gender, trans-occupational, trans-generational, trans-ethnic movement. It's impossible to build it with *only* young, strong, usually male people, however much we want them to be with us too. As one Italian woman wrote to me after the events: "As a citizen, I wish I had been in Genoa. But as a mother, I'm glad I wasn't."

In particular, immigrants and minority groups get hassled all the time by police anyway and they can't risk coming to demonstrations where there is a risk of confrontation as they will be the first to pay. Most trade unions are not going to join us either unless they can be sure that demonstrations will be without incidents like the ones that occurred in Genoa and Göteborg, where many small businesses and cars were trashed (some of them undoubtedly by police in disguise). We must oppose such property destruction particularly because it undermines the livelihoods or transport of ordinary people.

• Contrary to what the violent elements claim, violence against people or property strengthens rather than weakens capitalism.

These battles do not raise "class-consciousness"; they create, rather, mass sympathy for the objects of violence, whether hapless bank employees, car owners or police, by handing them the role of victims. Police, let's not forget, are overwhelmingly working class themselves. The cop who fired on Carlo Giuliani was a poor, virtually untrained twenty-one-year-old kid from Sicily who should never have been issued live ammunition. For him, joining the police was undoubtedly a social step upwards, much like joining the US army often is for young black Americans.

Some former Black Panthers including Bobby Seale recently got together in the United States to analyse the failure of their movement in the 1970s. They concluded that it was chiefly due to an escalation of violence which they could no longer control. If the political masters of the police do not want us to fail, then why do they order their cops to dress up as Black Bloc and start fights themselves?

Despite all these arguments, there are still genuine temptations to behave violently and these have to be recognised. Our American and Canadian friends mention them frequently in debates on the subject. Aside from the "structural violence of the system" arguments already given, they claim that in North America street violence is the only way to get media attention. One fine, experienced American activist wrote to me explaining that they had brought nearly 100.000 protesters to the Republican Party convention that nominated George Bush, but there was no violence and consequently no media coverage.

Some North American organisations, bending over backwards to be "inclusive" and "multicultural," and pushing "tolerance" to its outer limits, have adopted an approach they call "diversity of tactics." They argue that a variety of tactics, including violent ones, can coexist in the same demonstration. This slogan has unfortunately become a kind of cover for sectarian groups to "do their own thing."

A participant in the Quebec City demonstrations against the FTAA writes that diversity of tactics has become "simply a convenient mechanism for undermining the hard work of forging a solidarity movement." He gives the example of demonstrators who used a sit-in to block a supply route for the FTAA convention hall in Quebec. When they refused to leave, the police simply ordered their own infiltrators among the demonstrators to start throwing rocks, thus giving the police an excuse to charge. As they retreated, demonstrators saw the rock throwers jump into police vans and disappear.

As this young man says in his own colourful language, "I am more than willing to put my ass on the line for comrades but I will not face the gas, dogs, batons, rubber bullets, water cannons and boots all in order to provide cannon fodder for the diversity of tactics brigades which may in the end turn out to be cops."

Furthermore, and most importantly, "diversity of tactics" necessarily reflect the diversity of goals. The autonomy of each group around its chosen tactic guarantees there will be no unity in the demonstration and no clear message conveyed to the outside world.

Despite the commitment of nearly everyone in the movement to non-violent methods, despite large demonstrations in 2002 and 2003 unmarred by any negative incidents, we've still got to try to lay this ghost once and for all, because the problem can yet recur. We've got to improve "self-policing" methods and prevent violent elements from joining our demonstrations. What can be done?

First, one must make sure that the declared objective of the protest does not in itself *require* violence. Stopping the WTO meeting in Seattle for a whole day was accomplished by disciplined mass civil disobedience – but the venue was in the middle of the city in plain view. If you have a citadel as in Genoa or Quebec, surrounded by a physical wall plus a human wall of police, the goal of "stopping the meeting" in a non-violent way is no longer even thinkable. It's rather comparable to the lords of the manor inside the ramparts and the rabble milling about confusedly outside. One begins to wonder when the boiling oil will start to flow. Deafening noise might work in these cases but storming the walls certainly won't.

Especially in the United States and Canada, it has sometimes been possible to create a dialogue with Bloc people who have agreed not to disrupt demos. In Europe, few people seem to know exactly who to talk to, or at least I don't and I haven't met the people who do. Defenders of violence have upon occasion flooded my e-mail box with insults or pornography, but always anonymously. I'm undoubtedly too old. Younger people, if they agree with the arguments given here, ought to try.

We also need to reach them because they could conceivably evolve towards the kind of Red Brigades strategy which spelt death to the progressive movement in Germany and Italy in the 1970s. They are certainly physically courageous and we could undoubtedly use their courage in more constructive ways. If they are truly political, as they claim to be, it ought to be possible to debate with them, perhaps even to convince them that what they now propose is no solution for global poverty or environmental collapse and no way to undermine capitalism.

None of this means that protests have to be boring. Brazilians are fantastic at putting on colourful demos. A tradition of creative non-violence is especially lively in Britain, the United States and India. People can sign on for different degrees of engagement so that those willing to risk arrest for civil disobedience, like those who need to be sure they make it home the same evening, can participate in the same actions in different ways. Seattle was a model for halting a major meeting in a non-violent way, no matter how rough the cops' tactics or disruptive the actions of the spoilers. Instead of getting stuck in the violence debate, we must ask what tactics will be most effective in a given situation.

For years now I've dreamed about having a gigantic laugh-in ridiculing the "stupid white men" as Mike Moore would call them, these pretentious types who think they're anointed to rule the world. This would be my model for any future, hopefully last, G-8 meeting – last because they wouldn't dare meet again. Noise and thunderous, amplified, genuine laughter with thousands of people participating. With circus music. With clown suits. With masks of the 3-Bs, Bush, Berlusconi and

Blair, which in itself sounds like a comedy team. Since I first suggested this idea (with zero success), I learned that Indian activists had used a sit-down laugh-in against a particularly awful provincial government – and caused its downfall.

Particularly since September 11, the movement for global justice is at a turning point, one could even say on a razor's edge. The public mood has changed. Either we become a truly mass movement and therefore unstoppable, or we become marginalised, even criminalised, and the great globalisation juggernaut will catch up with us and crush us. It would not be the first time in history a promising movement failed, and we are not invulnerable.

This one has registered some stunning successes. On 15 February 2003, a remarkable and often-unheralded event took place: millions of people marched, with no violent incidents, in dozens of countries on the same day – before the war had even begun. The movement is now a power in itself even if it couldn't stop the war. For the first time, Europeans, Americans and countless others marched symbolically side by side with people in the Muslim world itself.

The movement has also clearly changed the terms of the debate and the issues it raises are now on the agenda. We are highly visible and our adversaries are obliged to take us more seriously, but we haven't actually won anything yet. We haven't obtained real debt cancellation, or profound reform (or abolition) of the World Bank, the IMF and the WTO, we haven't really slowed down speculation on financial markets nor won the battle for international taxation, we haven't got rid of tax havens or secured laws against abusive layoffs by profitable TNCs. In a word, transnational capitalism is standing fast.

Nonetheless, vast numbers of people have come to the conclusion that it is *possible* to do something against neo-liberal globalisation, whereas perhaps only five years ago they felt largely hopeless. Recognising this, the adversary will spend more time, energy and money to defeat us before we can push forward towards concrete victories. Criminalising the movement and its participants is one avenue towards that end. This is why, as I write this chapter, José Bové is once more in prison in the South of France.

We must either grow stronger or grow weaker and eventually become irrelevant. Only a broad, worldwide and long-term movement can accomplish what we have set out to do, something no one else has ever done in history.

Even if we are able to impose non-violence universally in our own ranks, we have no guarantees that the state will do the same. Indeed if we are at all successful in challenging the latest incarnation of capitalism, we must expect retaliation. The only answer to that is greater resistance, greater militancy, but above all *disciplined* militancy. Protests should be a sign that the movement is growing in numbers and in determination. Violence is a sign of weakness. Let us, rather, show the adversary our strength.

CONCLUSION
AND
SPEECH AT PORTO ALEGRE 2003

Proposals for change come with different degrees of difficulty and effort required to implement them. It's easier to prevent something new and awful from happening than to eliminate something old and awful that everyone has grown used to. Whatever the nature of the change one seeks, it's important to remember that since the dawn of humanity people have faced the same sneering opponents who pretend that what you want is unrealistic, utopian or impossible.

The principle vector of change today is neither political parties nor governmental leadership but the global justice movement seeking a very different kind of globalisation from the neo-liberal variety we've got. No one really knows why movements spring up when they do nor why they grow old and cold and wither away. I hope this book may contribute to keeping ours young and vibrant.

At the third annual rendezvous of the World Social Forum in 2003, I was asked to speak in the "Gigantinho," a well-deserved name as it seats about 15.000 people. The whole Porto Alegre process that year was to centre on strategies, because it was assumed the people attending had already identified the problems and had had enough of pointing accusing fingers. They also knew that plenty of proposals were on the table. The real problem was, and remains, the one I've tried, among others, to tackle here – how to turn proposals into reality.

As I finished this book, I learned that the Zapatista's Sub-comandante Marcos was probably the first to launch the slogan "another world is possible." Here, then, is credit where credit is due: Thank you Marcos. Although I did not realise you had supplied all but one word of the title, I hope my book is worthy of you. I hope too that you may find I have done justice to the "ifs."

I've been making suggestions throughout this book, itself a greatly extended version of my Porto Alegre speech. That's why, in lieu of a conclusion, I offer this speech in an edited version. It was part of a session on transnational corporations and financial markets.

Dear Friends and Comrades:

Look around you. It's a miracle that we should be together here at all. Even five years ago, no one, not even the most optimistic among us, could have imagined the size and scope of this movement. In historical terms, the four years since Seattle, the three gatherings here in Porto Alegre are nothing, a mere blink of an eye. What we have all accomplished in this brief moment is breathtaking. So we should see our presence here and the very existence of this movement and of the World Social Forum as a great victory.

The first gathering in Porto Alegre, in 2001, was intended to analyse the world situation. The second, in 2002, concentrated on proposals for alternatives. This year, we are supposed to be thinking about strategies for bringing about the changes we all hope for. So I will assume people here are aware of the basics on both transnational corporations, or TNCs, and financial markets. My real goal is to talk about strategies, not just concerning TNCs and financial markets but the strategies of the movement in general.

First, let's recognise that exhortation and persuasion will get us nowhere. It's no good repeating that this or that should or must happen. Wealth and power aren't listening and they never willingly share. Dominant classes do not give up their privileges. In fact, they always want more. Nothing is ever enough. Those in power will not protect the environment simply because it would be in everyone's interests to do so; they will continually try to confiscate the gains made by working people and they will not spontaneously help the poor however dire their situation may become. Let me put it bluntly: No level of human suffering, in and of itself, will cause either policy or behaviour to change.

Now I'm going to say some harsh, negative, even frightening things so before I do, let me say that despite everything, I am fundamentally hopeful. In the early twenty-first century, I believe we have crossed a threshold. Please allow me to refer to my own work to illustrate this point. Three years ago I wrote a book called *The Lugano Report*. When we speak here about the need for a radically different world, we have first to recognise the serious risk that the future world could be even worse than the one we've got if we don't prevent it. This is precisely the subject of the *Lugano Report*.

In this book I imagine that people very much like the ones meeting in Davos right now have commissioned a group of experts to write a report. The question the commissioners ask the experts is: "How can we preserve capitalism in the twenty-first century?" These Davos-like types want to make sure that capitalism will continue to dominate the world and thrive; how can they guarantee that it will be the only credible system, that no other can even be imagined? These "masters of the universe" want to know what they must do to keep themselves in power.

This is precisely the question we are asking here this evening, from precisely the opposite perspective. We are asking what must be done in order that the present capitalist order *not* prevail. What must we do to make sure that our lives and communities and natural environments are *not* ruled by the whims of corporations and financial markets?

The group of experts who are supposed to be writing the *Lugano Report* come to conclusions which are, to say the least, extremely unpleasant. For all kinds of reasons – economic, ecological, social and political – the expert group concludes that it will be altogether impossible to preserve capitalism in the year 2020 when there will be approximately eight billion human beings on earth. For that reason, a great many of those people, particularly the poorest ones, those who are not and cannot be integrated into the system, must be eliminated as quietly as possible and by whatever means may be necessary. War, famine and disease will be allowed to do their work and to take their toll.

The question we are asking in Porto Alegre, implicitly or explicitly, is therefore deadly serious. Can we or can we not change the present system, because if we cannot, then I deeply fear that the Lugano scenario is the one we shall be faced with. I believe we are now more starkly confronted with the horror of that scenario than ever before. If you think I'm exaggerating, look around. One symptom is the refusal to do anything serious about the ever-increasing AIDS crisis. AIDS is running wild in poor countries among poor people. AIDS is the Black Death of the twenty-first century …

Another Lugano-type symptom is the worsening of one conflict after another, with few efforts towards peaceful nego- tiated solutions. We all think first of Israel and Palestine, but there are in fact dozens of ongoing wars in the world right now. To give a single example, the Congo–Zaire war has already killed between three and four million people, no one knows quite how many.

Clearly the new teams in the White House and the Pentagon are using the attacks of September 11 to their advantage to justify the barbaric notion of "preventive" or "pre-emptive" war. Such wars, of which Iraq is likely to be only the first victim, will decimate civilian populations unless the peace movement can stop the American outlaws.

Famine too is once more on the rise. In the 1980s, govern- ments had promised to cut hunger in half by now from its levels of twenty years ago. Instead, more people are struck by food deprivation than ever before. The Director of the FAO recently said that at the rate we are going it will take 150 years to eliminate hunger altogether.

All this and much, much more gives me the feeling that the Lugano scenario is already being implemented. I don't mean there's a conspiracy because none is needed. The rich and pow- erful have apparently concluded, like the authors of my false report, that hundreds of millions of people in the world today are superfluous. They do not hold salaried jobs and they con- tribute nothing to capitalist production. They have little or no money and contribute nothing to capitalist consumption. They are not profitable, they are a drag on the economy and they are redundant.

There will be no Hitler–Auschwitz model because it's too visible, too expensive and creates resistance and eventually universal rejection. It is instead a postmodern, twenty-first-century model in which nothing can really be blamed on anyone. No one is responsible. Horrible things just happen and life goes on, at least for some.

Nothing, therefore, can be more serious than our struggle. If you share my analysis, as I hope you may, then clearly this gives all of us here an historic responsibility. In a word, we cannot fail. In the midst of this wonderful celebration in Porto Alegre, I hope we can also remain sober and thoughtful. The great nineteenth-century German philosopher G. W. F. Hegel said: "the only thing that history teaches us is that nobody ever learns anything from history."

Let's prove that Hegel was wrong and learn from history, which tells us that other movements of great promise have been destroyed in the past, either by their enemies or by their own mistakes. They too resisted the powerful, they too fought against the oppressors of their own times, they too held out great hopes for a different world. If they had won, then our own presence here in Porto Alegre and our own movement would be less necessary because the world would already be a decent place for everyone to live, a place without hunger or serious deprivation, where everyone would have a right to the basics of life. We would be living in harmony with the natural environment and would be governing our-selves according to democratic principles. This is sadly not the case.

We have to win the struggle this time, despite the fact that we are attempting to do something which our predecessors could not even dream of. We are trying to challenge neo-liberal corporate-led globalisation on its own terrain, the globe. So we must work not just in our local or national contexts, but inter-nationally as well. The ambition to build a truly global justice movement exists for the first time in human history.

Our adversaries, the transnational corporations, are a law unto themselves. Financial markets take no notice of the disasters they cause for ordinary people. International institutions like the World Bank, the International Monetary Fund and the World Trade Organisation are all engaged in *reducing* rather than expanding democratic spaces; they serve only those who are already profiting from the world system. So our movement will have to be a hundred times stronger and wiser and more determined than any other that has come before in creating those democratic spaces.

Make no mistake, however. The stronger we become, the more our enemies will seek to destroy us. This is only natural. In the world we want, these adversaries would lose everything: their power, their wealth, their prestige. So we must be alert to their strategies of destruction and not let down our guard.

Let's learn from history so that we don't also destroy ourselves. Fortunately I don't see any signs of this – quite the contrary. This young movement has shown startling maturity and has remained overwhelmingly non-violent. This is one reason we will surely be subjected to more provocations trying to incite us to violence. We must resist such provocations at all costs and never reproduce in our own ranks and our own practice the violence of our adversaries.

We need to learn. The first duty of the activist is to understand how the world works and how the institutions that oppress us function. Politics is more complicated than it used to be. When I started out, it was enough to say "US get out of Vietnam" and everyone understood what you were talking about. Today if you go out into the street and tell people about the WTO or the IMF, most of them won't have a clue what you're talking about. So we need to learn in order to be able to teach and to expand our movement.

We have also managed to run a democratic movement in the image of the democratic world we hope to create. This movement has moral, political and intellectual heroes and heroines and emblematic organisations we look up to; such individuals and groups inspire us but they do not, thank God, resemble the leadership in the corporate world. We have no one, nor do we want anyone, in a position to give orders and be obeyed. We are a network of networks. Let's make sure it stays that way.

Although part of our task is to make proposals for change, good proposals won't be accepted simply because they are good but only as a result of sustained pressure. The old ideas about changing the balance of forces and class struggle are still relevant. To change that balance, we need to forge alliances. The movement has so far been quite good at this, making common cause with ecologists, women's groups, small farmers, trade unions, development organisations, intellectual and cultural workers and now the peace movement, although there is still much room for improvement.

Still, in spite of these successes, we've not always been able to include the representatives of most disadvantaged people or most immigrant communities in our societies. The movement remains on the whole middle class so we must try to reach out to those people who need a different world even more than we do but who are concentrating most of the time on their own survival.

So far, wherever our adversaries have gathered, we've been there. We have comrades protesting against the financial and corporate elites in Davos at this very moment. I think we now need to agree on the following principle: wherever they are, *some* of us will be, but only some of us, usually the people who are geographically closest to the venue. Some of us but not all, because many of us can't afford to travel or can't afford to be away from their jobs or their families.

Furthermore, some activists closest to the grass-roots are also the poorest and they aren't necessarily in Porto Alegre or at the other major venues of the movement. How can we share limited material resources with them? Should we start thinking about fundraising in order to bring in the real grass-roots? Many funders are by now sympathetic to our goals.

Occasionally, we need to impress the media with numbers. The European Social Forum in Florence in November 2002 was one such occasion and it was a tremendous experience to march for peace and justice with a million people. Nonetheless, we need to find new ways to express our opposition, and this can often be done with relatively few people.

I've already said that non-violence must be our guiding principle. However, peaceful doesn't mean boring. We need to attract attention with more artistic expression, more colour, more creativity and we can learn an enormous amount from the Brazilians in this regard. Let's remember as well that the people we're protesting against are not just contemptible, they're ludicrous. One of my dreams is to be a part of several thousand people just laughing at these pretentious types.

Journalists constantly ask if we shouldn't become a political party. For me, the answer is emphatically "No!" We are deeply political and we must therefore work partly through politicians and parties but do our politics differently from them. I don't mean this as an insult, but traditional politics is the place of compromise. That is simply the nature of the beast. Even when one of our own, like Lula, takes power, he still needs an independent movement to push his government.

We can't always or even often act directly on the international sphere because there are no democratic spaces open to us at that level. So we must exercise influence at the local and national levels where at least some space exists. Surely we should seize them and push our governments towards adopting our proposals. How can we change or abolish the World Trade Organisation, the IMF, the World Bank if not through governments? Stopping the occasional meeting through protests may be a highly symbolic success but it does not kill the institution. We need binding laws.

One of our chief problems is that much of the international law that exists has been made by and for the transnationals and the financial markets. Without laws, we'll have to repeat Seattle, and for that matter Porto Alegre, for the rest of the century. The WTO can make law but the movement has no way of doing so unless it uses governments.

We need to create spaces in which genuine political and economic experiments and change can take place. Some say that proposals for international taxation or shutting down tax havens or cancelling debt are merely reformist, not worth fighting for, not revolutionary enough. I disagree. If implemented, such proposals would be truly revolutionary because they would introduce a qualitative change; just as national taxation and redistribution changed wealth distribution patterns in countries that adopted them. The proof is that every time the right-wing comes back to power, it immediately lowers taxes on the rich and on corporations.

Let me end on a personal note. Since the days of the anti-Vietnam war movement, I have never been so hopeful. Let me affirm here my deep conviction that the future of the global justice movement is bright. This movement no longer depends on the personal presence or absence of this person or that person, no matter who they are. It has taken on a life of its own; it has become healthy, self-sustaining and it is developing like a living organism with no part in competition with the others or superseding the others.

Since we are privileged to participate in this unique gathering of the World Social Forum, let's remember that such privilege carries responsibility. Never forget that we are all actors in history. We are linked to the past and we have a duty to be worthy of those who came before us, that innumerable legion who fought poverty, injustice and oppression with the tools of their own times. We, in this brilliant and fortunate moment here in Porto Alegre, are also a bond and a promise to the future, through our hope, our daily work and our determination as we proclaim "Another world is possible."

Now let's make it.

NOTES

1. Geminiano Montanari (1633–1687) *Della Moneta, Trattato Mercantile* quoted by Marx from an 1804 edition, in the *Critique de l'Economie Politique*, La Pléiade, ed., *Economie I*, p. 414. I first found it in a piece by Gilbert Rist.

2. Clifford Lamberg-Karlovsky quoted in "You don't get many of those to the shekel," *New Scientist*, 26 May 2001, p. 20; see also *Nature*, vol. 411, p. 487.

3. United Nations, *World Investment Report 2002*, Box and Table IV. 1, p. 90. This list is based on "value added," a more accurate measure than just "sales," on which some previous lists compiled by other sources relied. By 1995, when sales-only methodology was used, there were already forty-nine countries but fifty-one firms on the list.

4. I have hunted high and low for my printed source on this quote and not found it. But in 2002 I was in a debate with Mr. Barnevik in Salzburg where I quoted in public this declaration. He neither protested nor denied it, so I assume it's accurate.

5. United Nations, *World Investment Report 2002*, p. 118.

6. Manuel Castells, "Internet and Internet Society," contribution to the catalogue of El Primer Festival de Arte, Ciencia

y Technologia, Dinamicas Fluidas, Madrid 2002.

7. Economist John Williamson, then with the Inter-American Development Bank, is generally credited with inventing the term "Washington Consensus."

8. Mark Weisbrot, Dean Baker, Egor Kraev, Judy Chen, "The Scorecard on Globalization 1980–2000: 20 years of diminished progress," Center for Economic and Policy Research, July 2001. Highly recommended.

9. See Mark Buchanan, "That's the Way the Money Goes," *New Scientist*, 19 August 2000.

10. Giovanni Andrea Cornia, "Liberalization, Globalization and Income Distribution," UN University-WIDER (World Institute for Development Economic Research) Working Paper no. 157, Helsinki, March 1999.

11. Sanjay G. Reddy and Thomas W. Pogge, "How *Not* to Count the Poor," 1 May 2002, available pending publication online at www.socialanalysis.org.

12. Charte Sécurité Environment de TotalFina: "Acune priorité économique ne s'exerce au détriment de la sécurité dans le travail ou du respect de l'environnement .... Le Groupe choisit ses partenaires industriels et commerciaux en fonction de leur aptitude à adhérer aux règles de Total en matrière de sécurité et d'environnement," signed Thierry Demarest, President.

13. Adam Smith does not develop these ideas much in the *Wealth of Nations* but in the *Theory of Moral Sentiments*.

14. Garrett Hardin, "The Tragedy of the Commons," *Science*, vol. 162, pp. 1243–8, 13 December 1968.

15. For a good collection of studies about common property arrangements, see Michael Goldman, ed., *Privatizing Nature: Political Struggles for the Global Commons*, Transnational Institute and Pluto Press: London 1998.

My preface to this volume is available on my website: www.tni.org/george.

16. Larry Summers in an interview with Kirstin Garrett, journalist with the Australian Broadcasting Company, broadcast on the Australian national radio programme "Background Briefing" on 10 November 1991 and transcribed here from the tape.

17. Wilfred Beckerman, *Small is Stupid: Blowing the Whistle on the Greens*, Duckworth: London 1995, published the following year in the US by the right-wing libertarian Cato Institute under the title *Through Green-Colored Glasses.*

18. P. M. Vitousek, P. R. Ehrlich and P. A. Matson, "Human appropriation of the products of photosynthesis," *Bioscience*, vol. 36, 1986, p. 368–73. This team's figures and analysis were reconfirmed by S. Rojstaczer, S. M. Sterling and N. J. Moore, "Human appropriation of photosynthesis products," *Science*, no. 294, 2001, p. 2549sq.

19. See Mathis Wackernagel and William Rees, *Our Ecological Footprint*, New Society Publishers: Gabriola Island, BC, Canada and Philadelphia, PA, 1996.

20. See the site www.global-vision.org/city/footprint.html.

21. Patrick Viveret, *Les Nouveaux Facteurs de Richesse* and *Reconsidérons la Richesse*, transversal.apinc.org or www.place-publique.fr/esp/richesse/index.html.

22. Susan George and Fabrizio Sabelli, *Faith and Credit: The World Bank's Secular Empire*, Penguin and Westview Press: 1995.

23. David Hartridge, "What the General Agreement on Trade in Services (GATS) Can Do," speaking at the symposium held by the international law firm Clifford Chance on "Opening markets for banking worldwide" in 1997.

24. Renato Ruggiero (then director general of the WTO)

speaking at the meeting on 2 July 1998 of the Conference on Trade in Services in Brussels, organised by the European Commission.

25. Franz Boas, *The Social Organisation and the Secret Societies of the Kwakiutle Indians*, 1897.

26. United Nations, *World Investment Report 2002*, Table IV. 2, p. 89.

27. Ibid., citing the auditing firm PriceWaterhouseCoopers, p. 132.

28. Part of the information about overcapacity in the automobile industry and this example are drawn from Willam Greider's excellent book *One World, Ready or Not*, Simon & Schuster: New York 1997.

29. Ibid, p. 119.

30. United Nations, *World Investment Report 2002*, Table I. 3, p. 12.

31. Joseph E. Stiglitz, *Globalization and its Discontents*, W. W. Norton: New York 2002.

32. Corporate European Observatory, *Europe Inc.*, Amsterdam, May 1997; updated and enlarged edition, Pluto Press: London 2000.

33. Baron Daniel Janssen, "The Pace of Economic Change in Europe," speech to the annual general assembly of the Trilateral Commission, Tokyo, April 2000; see www.trilateral.org.

34. Periodically the Federal Register, on behalf of the US Special Trade Representative, invites submissions from interested members of the public on USTR policy. These are public documents and may be consulted on the site of the USCSI. These submissions are extremely revealing of the sorts of things service industries hope to gain in WTO or regional trade agreements. See for example the

Coalition's site www.uscsi.org: US Coalition of Service Industries, Services 2000 USTR Federal Register Submission, "Response to Federal Register Notice of August 19, 1998, Solicitations of Public Comment Regarding US Preparations for the World Trade Organization's Ministerial Meeting, Fourth Quarter, 1999" and subsequent responses.

35. Susan George, "Vers une offensive américaine sur less OGM" and "Personne ne veut des OGM, sauf les industriel," *Le Monde diplomatique*, May 2002 and April 2003.

36. See the *Greenpeace Guide to Anti-Environmental Organisations*, Odonian Press: Berkeley, CA, 1993.

37. www.esf.org.

38. Compare the declarations of the International Chamber of Commerce such as Chambre de Commerce Internationale, *Déclaration présentée aux chefs d'État et de gouvernement au sommet de Cologne du 18–20 juin 1999*, "Les Enterprises et l'Economie Mondiale," 11 mai 1999, also ICC, *World Business Priorities for the Second Ministerial Conference of the World Trade Organisation*, doc. 103/202, 3 April 1998, with those of the European Commission (i.e. of Sir Leon Brittan): Note for the 133 Committee, 26 April 1999, Subject: EU Trade Ministers Informal Meeting, Berlin 9–10 May 1999; and Sir Leon Brittan, "The Contribution of the WTO Millennium Round to Globalisation: an EU View," speech for the Herbert Batliner Symposium, "Europe in the Era of Globalisation, Economic Order and Economic Law," Vienna, 29 April 1999.

39. In my doctoral thesis, I analysed Nestlé's spurious claims and shoddy research which tried to prove that its products and practices did not increase infant mortality and

morbidity in the Third World; published as *Les Stratèges de la Faim*, Editions Grounauer: Geneva 1981.

40. Christian Losson, et al., "Messes basses entre maîtres du monde," *Libération*, 5 August 2003. Various websites deal with Bilderberg (the name of the hotel where it first met fifty years ago – now it changes locations) but no one except the participants really knows who's there and what they talk about.

41. See Walt Kelly, *The Pogo Papers 1952–53* or the *Best of Pogo*, Simon and Schuster: New York 1982.

42. An excellent book on this subject is Matt Ridley, *The Origins of Virtue*, Viking: New York 1996.

43. William Pfaff: "White House Message: Refusing to treat allies as equals," *International Herald Tribune*, 7 July 2003.

44. Melanie Beth Oliviero and Adele Simmons tell this story in Chapter 4 of Marlies Glasius, Mary Kaldor and Helmut Anheier, eds, *Global Civil Society 2002*, Oxford University Press: 2002.

45. The Fox News story is one of eighteen concerning award-winning journalists whose stories were killed: Kristina Borjesson, ed., *Into the Buzzsaw* (Foreword by Gore Vidal), Prometheus Books: New York 2002.

46. Jeane Kirkpatrick, "Establishing a Viable Human Rights Policy," paper delivered at the Kenyon College Human Rights Conference, 4 April 1981.

47. Michael Benton, *When Life Nearly Died: The Greatest Mass Extinction Of All Time*, Thames and Hudson: London 2003; George Monbiot's article, "Shadow of Extinction," appeared in the *Guardian* of 1 July 2003.

48. See Monbiot, ibid; also Robert Watson, *Report to the Sixth Conference*, United Nations Framework Convention on Climate Change, 20 November 2000.

49. See Fred Pearce, "An Ordinary Miracle," *New Scientist*, 3 February 2001.

50. Michael Albert, *Parecon: Life after Capitalism*, Verso: London and New York 2003.

51. See the International Forum on Globalization, www.ifg.org, several authors, *A Better World is Possible*, 2002.

52. See *Forbes*, 17 March 2003.

53. Greg Palast, *The Best Democracy Money Can Buy*, Pluto Press: London and Sterling, VA, 2002.

54. The World Bank's *Operations Evaluation Department Report* of March 2003.

55. See the statistics drawn from official sources succinctly presented on the site of the Comité pour l'annulation de la dette du Tiers Monde (Committee for the Cancellation of Third World Debt), www.cadtm.org, in French but easy to understand.

56. Susan George, *How the Other Half Dies: The real reasons for world hunger*, Penguin and Allanheld, Osmun: 1976.

57. My thesis, defended in 1978 at the Sorbonne and given the highest mention ("très honorable"), was later published in Switzerland thanks to the interest of the then director of the IUED, Roy Preiswerk. Susan George, *Les Stratèges de la Faim*, Grounauer with the Institut Universitaire d'Études de Développement, eds, University of Geneva, 1981.

58. Thomas Kuhn, *The Structure of Scientific Revolutions*, Harvard University Press: Cambridge, MA, 1962, rev. 1979.

59. I dealt with this question more fully in "Winning the War of Ideas," *Dissent*, Summer 1997, also on my website.

60. Susan George and Fabrizio Sabelli, *Faith and Credit: The World Bank's Secular Empire*.

61. Susan George, *The Lugano Report*, Pluto Press: London 1999.
62. See www.tni.org/george for my own illusions.
63. Justin Podur, "Consumption, Complicity and SUVBs," the ZNet Commentary for 29 December 2001.